ASSISTED SUICIDE AND EUTHANASIA:
Christian Moral Perspectives
The Washington Report

◼

Committee on Medical Ethics
Episcopal Diocese of Washington
Episcopal Church House
Mount Saint Alban
Washington, D.C. 20016

◼

*Adopted at the Diocesan Convention
on January 25, 1997*

MOREHOUSE PUBLISHING

Morehouse Publishing

P.O. Box 1321
Harrisburg, PA 17105

A catalog record for this book is available from the Library of Congress.

Printed in the United States of America

Table of Contents

2. God's purposes
    a. God's purposes and sovereignty would still be honored if assisted suicide/euthanasia were allowed
    b. Assisted suicide/euthanasia are appropriate moral responses to pain and suffering
3. The impact of contemporary medicine
    a. To curb the unrelenting power of medical technology we must use assisted suicide/euthanasia
    b. An analogy with the rightness of decisions to withdraw treatment supports assisted suicide/euthanasia
    c. Physicians appropriately participate in assisted suicide/euthanasia
4. The social context
    a. The dangers of assisted suicide/euthanasia to the community can be overcome
    b. Precautions can be taken against financial coercion of the critically ill into assisted suicide/euthanasia
5. Concluding statement on accepting assisted suicide/euthanasia

1. God's purposes
    a. God's purposes would be impeded and God's sovereignty violated if assisted suicide/euthanasia were condoned
    b. Some pain and suffering is inevitable; we are called to alleviate it through morally acceptable means, rather than by killing
2. Human choice
    a. Christian moral constraints on autonomy work against allowing assisted suicide/euthanasia
    b. The availability of assisted suicide/euthanasia would eliminate our choice to remain alive without having to justify our existence
3. The impact of contemporary medicine
    a. Appropriate treatment of pain and suffering would decrease requests for assisted suicide/euthanasia

b. The role of the physician is to heal, not to kill
c. Other means can be used to respond to the overuse of medical technology than assisted suicide/euthanasia
4. The social context
  a. Assisted suicide/euthanasia present individuals and society with dangers of abuse
  b. Some persons would be pressured to end their lives for financial reasons if assisted suicide/euthanasia were available
  c. The social isolation of the dying, as well as the elderly and some with disabilities, may lead them inappropriately to choose assisted suicide/euthanasia
5. Concluding statement on rejecting assisted suicide/euthanasia

Acknowledgements

The Committee on Medical Ethics of the Diocese of Washington owes a tremendous debt of gratitude to the following persons who generously devoted a great deal of time to reviewing an earlier draft of this report.

Elise Ayers, M.P.H., Center to Improve the Care of the Dying, George Washington University, Washington, D.C.

Richard Beatty, J.D., law firm of Shaw, Pittman, Potts, and Trowbridge, Washington, D.C.

Tom L. Beauchamp, Ph.D., Kennedy Institute of Ethics, Georgetown University, Washington, D.C.

The Rev. Joan Beilstein, Director of Pastoral Care and Chaplain, Manor Care Health Services at Fair Oaks, Virginia

Ellen W. Bernal, Ph.D., Hospital ethicist, St. Vincent Medical Center, Toledo, Ohio

James F. Childress, Ph.D., Chair, Religious Studies, University of Virginia, Charlottesville, Virginia

Barbara Springer Edwards, R.N., MTS, Director, Cardiac Surgical Unit, Alexandria Hospital, Alexandria, Virginia

Margaret Farley, Ph.D., Yale Divinity School, New Haven, Connecticut

Marcia Day Finney, Ph.D., Humanities in Medicine, University of Virginia Health Sciences Center, Charlottesville, Virginia

Elizabeth Fisher, Ph.D., Chair, Classical Studies, George Washington University, Washington, D.C.

Leslie Pickering Francis, Ph.D., J.D., Law and Philosophy, University of Utah, Salt Lake City, Utah

The Rt. Rev. Ronald H. Haines, Bishop of Washington, Mount St. Alban, Washington, D.C.

Elizabeth Heitman, Ph.D., Program on Humanities and
Technology in Health Care, School of Public Health,
University of Texas, Houston, Texas

The Rev. Dr. Jan C. Heller, Director, Center for Ethics in
Health Care, Atlanta, Georgia

Bruce Jennings, Executive Director, The Hastings Center,
Briarcliff Manor, New York

The Rt. Rev. Terence Kelshaw, Bishop of the Rio Grande,
Albuquerque, New Mexico

Elizabeth Leland, economist, Burke, Virginia

The Rev. Theodore Lewis, Germantown, Maryland

Joanne Lynn, M.D., Center to Improve the Care of the Dying,
George Washington University Medical Center,
Washington, D.C.

Elizabeth McCloskey, M.T.S., Falls Church, Virginia

The Rev. Loren Mead, President emeritus, The Alban Institute,
Washington, D.C.

The Rev. Dr. E.F. Michael Morgan, Rector, Church of the
Good Shepherd, Athens, Ohio

The Rev. Dr. John Morgan, St. John's College, St. Lucia,
Australia

The Rev. Margaret Muncie, Chaplain, the Dupree Community,
Cincinnati, Ohio

The Rev. Allan M. Parrent, Ph.D., Virginia Theological
Seminary, Alexandria, Virginia

Stephen Post, Ph.D., Center for Biomedical Ethics, Case
Western Reserve University School of Medicine, Cleveland,
Ohio

The Rev. Dr. Charles Price, Virginia Theological Seminary,
Alexandria, Virginia

The Rt. Rev. Kenneth L. Price, Suffragan Bishop, Diocese of
Southern Ohio, Columbus, Ohio

Don Reed, Ph.D., Philosophy, Wittenberg University,
Springfield, Ohio

Augusta Rowe, seminarian, Virginia Theological Seminary,
Alexandria, Virginia

The Rev. Dr. David A. Scott, Virginia Theological Seminary,
Alexandria, Virginia

Timothy Sedgwick, Ph.D., Seabury-Western Theological Seminary, Evanston, Illinois

David Smith, Ph.D., The Poynter Center for the Study of Ethics and American Institutions, Indiana University, Bloomington, Indiana

The Rev. Dr. Harmon L. Smith, Divinity School, Duke University, Durham, North Carolina

Martin L. Smith, S.T.D., Department of Bioethics, Cleveland Clinic Foundation, Cleveland, Ohio

The Rt. Rev. Stephen Sykes, Bishop of Ely, Cambridgeshire, England

The Rev. Dr. Alan C. Tull, Rector, St. Mary's Church, Provo, Utah

The Very Rev. P. Linwood Urban, Ph.D., Chair and professor emeritus, Department of Religion, Swarthmore College, Swarthmore, Pennsylvania

Nancy Urban, M.S.W., Swarthmore, Pennsylvania

Robert M. Veatch, Ph.D., Kennedy Institute of Ethics, Georgetown University, Washington, D.C.

The Rev. Dr. Francis H. Wade, Rector, St. Alban's Church, Washington, D.C.

The Very Rev. George L.W. Werner, Dean, Trinity Cathedral, Pittsburgh, Pennsylvania

The Rev. Pierre Whalon, Rector, St. Andrew's Episcopal Church and School, Fort Pierce, Florida

Ann Yarborough, M.T.S., Arlington, Virginia

We are grateful to Patricia N. Timberlake for help with the design of the report. We would also like to thank the Endowment for Mission and Ministry of St. Paul's Episcopal Church, Indianapolis, Indiana, for financial assistance for a broader project, *Toward a Good Christian Death*, from which material for this report was drawn, and an anonymous donor for funds that enabled us to print this report. It should be understood that the Committee on Medical Ethics of the Diocese of Washington is entirely responsible for the material presented in this report and that our reviewers and funders do not necessarily endorse all of the views stated here. ■

Executive Summary

The Committee on Medical Ethics of the Diocese of Washington believes that the Episcopal Church must engage in a thorough discussion of the pressing question of assisted suicide and euthanasia for those near death who are in pain and suffering. The committee, which represents a range of moral positions about these acts, believes that its internal differences about this matter reflect the moral situation of many in the church today. Therefore, in this report, the committee presents both sides of the question, as well as two "middle" views, to assist Episcopalians and the larger Christian and secular societies to grasp more fully what these practices put at stake, morally and theologically. The basic question the committee asks in this report is whether new knowledge or circumstances give us reason to change the long-standing Christian prohibition against assisted suicide and euthanasia.

After defining key terms and distinctions, the committee presents views of suicide and euthanasia that have been handed down within the Christian tradition. It also considers whether that tradition requires Christians to extend our lives for as long as possible to uphold the sanctity of human life. Next, the committee presents the major Christian and relevant secular arguments for and against assisted suicide and euthanasia. Both sets of arguments consider such matters as God's purposes and sovereignty, respect for self-determination, Christian moral constraints on individual choice, appropriate Christian responses to pain and suffering, ways in which to limit medical technology, the role of physicians at the end of life, and the dangers of assisted suicide and euthanasia to the community and to those who are critically ill, poor, disabled, or otherwise vulnerable. The report also explores two "middle" approaches to the morality of assisted suicide and euthanasia, one of which excuses and the other of which justifies these acts in certain rare, extreme circumstances. In the course of examining these arguments, the committee considers whether we as a society can and should do more to provide adequate comfort care for those who are in pain and suffering and near death.

In the final section of the report, the committee notes that those Christians who accept and those who reject assisted suicide and euthanasia share certain convictions. Both have a sense of the sovereignty of God; both want to protect human dignity and individual freedom to choose how to confront human finitude and death; both view life as a good in relationship to the broader purposes of life; both recognize that human life, especially in situations of death and dying, can confront us with a conflict between physical life and other purposes or goods of life; both feel compassion toward those who suffer at the end of life. Moreover, both recognize that Christian principles of social justice call us to remedy a public policy that provides inadequate social support to the poor and very sick, as well as to those who are better off financially, yet lack medical and social resources during illness.

The central differences between those who favor and those who oppose assisted suicide and euthanasia lie in (1) the judgment they make about God's purposes and power in light of human suffering and (2) their evaluation of whether adequate safeguards can be built into a policy of assisted suicide/euthanasia. First, those who accept assisted suicide/euthanasia maintain that God's dominion over our lives does not require us to continue to live in pain and suffering, but allows us to assist those near death to go on to eternal life quickly and directly. Those who are critical of assisted suicide/euthanasia maintain that our stewardship over life does not include the choice to directly end it. Rather than kill, they believe, we must withdraw useless treatment and provide adequate pain relief and compassionate care and comfort to the dying. Second, Christian proponents of assisted suicide and euthanasia believe that strong and effective protections can be written into policies allowing these practices. Opponents, pointing to the experience of the Netherlands, maintain that such safeguards cannot be guaranteed and implemented and that once we start down the path that accepts killing, we will be impelled to extend it to the most vulnerable among us.

Although some might have preferred that the Committee on Medical Ethics reach morally binding conclusions, we have not yet found a way to do so at this time. Instead, we think we can serve the church best by examining these issues through a balanced approach that will illuminate them anew. We believe that this document offers a necessary step in the church's process of discernment of the way God would have us respond to the poignant and divisive matters of assisted suicide and euthanasia. We suggest that the final approach that the church takes to assisted suicide and euthanasia should lead us to take account of the underlying, broader question concerning care for the critically ill and dying: How can we enable one another to die a good Christian death? ■

Introduction

1. The question at issue

We have always had the ability to commit suicide or request euthanasia in times of serious illness—that is, intentionally to take our own lives to end our pain and suffering or to have others do this for us. Yet these acts have been prohibited within the Christian tradition from early times. Is there reason to change this prohibition today? This question, in turn, engages a larger one: How can we help one another to die a good Christian death? Our attempts to respond to these questions, ironically, have been made more difficult by the very medical advances we thought would resolve them.

Ours is a culture caught up in the attempt to conquer death. We have put tremendous energy into developing medical practices and technologies that might overcome it. Yet we are beginning to realize that the medical arsenal we have amassed to battle death also carries with it the power to propel us into a prolonged, painful, and lingering death. Moreover, our fascination with conquering death has left us with few means to cope with what we perceive as our "failures"—those who, despite our best efforts, are close to death. We lack the will and resources needed to provide appropriate comfort and support to many who are dying.

As we see some relatives and friends kept alive too long in poor condition by the use of medical powers, we wonder whether it would not be better to provide them with a quick and merciful death. Are assisted suicide and euthanasia compassionate and Christian responses to those in pain and suffering who face death? Or are they ways of isolating and abandoning them, of fleeing from compassion for those who are near death, rather than expressing it? Indeed, are there some alternative ways for

Christians to view the use of assisted suicide and euthanasia for the seriously ill and dying?

2. The genesis and range of this report

The Committee on Medical Ethics of the Episcopal Diocese of Washington here addresses the issue of assisted suicide/euthanasia as part of a larger report we have been developing, entitled, *Toward A Good Christian Death*. We believe that an adequate examination of the morality of assisted suicide and euthanasia requires exploring a whole set of moral and social questions about appropriate and compassionate care near the end of life.

We were stimulated to develop this separate document by the 1996 *Report of the Task Force on Assisted Suicide of the Diocese of Newark*.[1] In that report, the Newark Task Force stated that committing suicide or helping someone to do so may be morally acceptable for Christians under some circumstances. The members of the Task Force and the Bishop of Newark are to be commended for addressing an issue which, because of its potential for controversy, other dioceses might be inclined to avoid. This matter cries out for religious contributions and perspectives. The *Newark Report* responded to that need. Yet there are significant questions that were not considered in the *Newark Report* and issues that need clarification.

Consequently, we believe the Episcopal Church must engage in an even more thorough exploration of the morality of assisted suicide and euthanasia so that its members and many in the larger society might better grasp what is at stake, morally and theologically. This study is designed to do just that. It offers arguments for and against assisted suicide and euthanasia, as well as two other approaches. In addition, it provides an analysis of the long-range effects these practices might have on our community if they were adopted as a matter of public policy. Moreover, it addresses the question whether we as a society could do more to provide adequate comfort care for those who are suffering and in pain at the end of their lives. We offer this report for study and reflection by Episcopal laypersons and clergy, Christians generally, the terminally ill and their families, health caregivers, government policy makers, and those with an interest in the issues.

We have tried to include every Christian rationale and relevant secular rationales we could conceive of or find, for and against assisted suicide/euthanasia. We found more arguments in the literature against these practices than for them, since the former view has been the dominant one throughout the history of the Church. Our study reflects this uneven situation. The resulting greater number of arguments against these practices found in this report, however, should not be taken by the reader to indicate that our committee has reached a final conclusion on the question. Our committee represents a range of positions about the morality of assisted suicide/euthanasia. This has led us to attempt to give a fair and reasoned treatment of the significant rationales behind the various views enunciated by Christians. Although some might have preferred that we reach morally binding conclusions, we have not yet found a way to do so. Instead, we believe we are called to examine these issues by means of a balanced approach that will illuminate them anew. We hope in this way to move people of faith toward a conclusion that can be supported by Scripture, reason, and tradition.

St. Paul encouraged the early church to consider "disputable matters" (Romans 14:1) in terms that would "build up" the community. The contemporary church is also called to reflection today as a concrete expression of our love for God and one another—the love that formed the wellspring of Christ's own life. We are called to discern in what way God would have the church respond to the poignant and divisive matters of assisted suicide and euthanasia. This document offers a necessary step in this process of discernment. We hope readers will use it as a resource in attempting to learn how God would have us move in this matter. We invite Episcopalians and other interested persons within and without the Christian tradition to join us in this effort.

3. The Christian tradition and the Anglican moral vision

Christians cannot avoid the issue of physician-assisted suicide and euthanasia. It has been brought into prominence by the trials of Dr. Jack Kevorkian, the decision of the Supreme Court to review two recent Federal Courts of Appeals holdings in favor of assisted suicide, and stories about "mercy killings" and disputed treatment withdrawals highlighted in T.V. newscasts and newspaper head-lines. Christians naturally look to the Church, as the upholder of a moral tradition and provider of pastoral care, for guidance on this matter.

It is appropriate to do so, for Christians bring a distinctive theological and moral framework to these questions. Moreover, we bring centuries of experience of seeking both meaningful death and meaningful life in death's shadow. We are grounded in the conviction that the whole sum and purpose of our existence is to respond to God's call to a loving relationship with the Creator, Sustainer, and Redeemer of life. Our Christian understanding of the moral life is embedded in that relationship and looks to the transformation of our character through the imitation of Christ. Christians are called by God as a community to embody relations of trust, care, and mutual dependence. In short, there are certain ends that shape the way Christians should live—and the way we should die.

Anglican moralists, while adopting many traditional Christian moral principles and distinctions, have not set up an authoritative "system" of teachings[2] to apply to the question of the morality of assisted suicide/euthanasia. They appeal to Scripture, tradition, and reason as complementary guides in morals, belief, and worship.[3] No one of these alone, however, is taken by the Anglican tradition as the exclusive basis for moral action. Scripture, tradition, and reason are interwoven to create a rich tapestry that leads us to develop a sense of what conclusion is fitting to the moral question at hand.[4]

More specifically, Anglicanism can be viewed, over the course of its history, as embracing a moral vision grounded in several fea-tures:[5]

• One is that there is an objective moral order in creation that is grounded in God's wisdom. Through God's gift of moral rea-son, we can perceive and understand something of this moral order. Anglicanism does not ignore flaws in our powers of moral perception and reasoning, but it also recognizes that God moves in us and calls us back to a moral life when we err.

•   A second feature is a concern for love and justice, undergirded by the belief that each person, as a creature who reflects the image of God, has great worth as an individual and member of the community. The core of our dignity lies in our relation to God,[6] not in such characteristics as our intelligence or ability to make free choices.

•   Third, the moral life, in Anglicanism, does not consist simply of the attitudes and intentions of individuals, but has a social dimension grounded in our unity in the body of Christ. This calls us to take seriously the values of family, church, and community.

•   Fourth, living the moral life is an essential aspect of our relation to God. It is, in a sense, a sharing in the divine life itself, not merely a response to what God has done for us. Hooker attested that God has "deified our nature, though not by turning it into himself, yet by making it his own inseparable habitation."[7]

These, then, are several general—and yet significant—features of the Anglican moral vision that we bring to the question whether to revise the traditional Christian prohibition against assisted suicide and euthanasia. They require us to struggle not only with the question of how to express love and compassion for valuable human beings who are very ill and dying, but how to do so within the bounds of God's just purposes and the common good. They lead us to suggest that two conditions would need to be met if we were to justify altering the guidance that the church has offered about assisted suicide and euthanasia:

1)   new knowledge or circumstances would arise relevant to assisted suicide and euthanasia and

2)   in view of these, fundamental Christian moral values and principles would demand a revision of the traditional position that assisted suicide and euthanasia are wrong. ■

Contemporary Factors Which Have Prompted a Second Look at Assisted Suicide and Euthanasia

Have new knowledge or circumstances arisen relevant to assisted suicide and euthanasia? Certain features of contemporary life have propelled some to reexamine the traditional Christian position regarding assisted suicide and euthanasia. At least six striking aspects of our life and culture today have given a powerful impetus to this reconsideration.

1. A greater emphasis on personal self-determination and autonomy

Thirty or forty years ago, physicians made medical decisions for their patients, acting out of the benevolent desire to heal and comfort them. In recent years, however, we have reacted against such medical paternalism, and now strongly emphasize individual self-determination and informed consent.[8] The right to "death with dignity," which leans heavily on respect for personal autonomy, has become a clarion call of the patients' rights movement.

2. A growing drive to control death

Our newly honed medical and technological powers give us greater control today than ever before over when and how we die. Yet our medical capabilities, instead of conquering death, have only shifted the causes of death in developed countries. These have changed from infectious diseases, such as cholera, typhoid fever, and dysentery, to degenerative diseases, such as stroke, heart disease, and dementia.[9] Consequently, today we can draw out a dying process that would have been fairly quick in the past. We have made it possible to die in pieces. As a result, the question of how long life should be sustained by medical advances is increasingly being raised.

3. A fear of dying in pain and suffering

Some of us fear dying in pain and suffering as much as we fear death. This is so even though the development of anesthetics, morphine derivatives, and barbiturates in the last century and a half would seem to make possible a relatively painless death. It is the case even though the hospice movement has developed ways to relieve extreme suffering caused not only by physical pain, but by emotional anguish. Despite these advances, studies show that physicians generally are not well informed about available techniques for controlling pain and lessening suffering in those who are terminally ill.[10] Consequently, they tend in general not to offer adequate relief to the dying.

4. The institutionalization of dying

The overwhelming majority of Americans die in institutional settings, such as nursing homes and hospitals. While some of these offer care, safety, and familiar personnel and surroundings, others represent sterile and public environments. Patients and residents in the latter may encounter a form of alienation and depersonalization in which their physical, emotional, and spiritual needs are not met.[11] They may feel trapped and abandoned to strangers. Often they cannot return home because no one is there who can care for them. Thus, dying can come to mean isolation and abandonment for some in our society who live in institutions.

5. Novel economic pressures

It costs too much to try to avoid death today. Because treatment of the very ill may take a long time, and may be accompanied by the use of exotic medical technologies or of long-term custodial care, it can be expensive. Individuals with private health care insurance who need treatment beyond that covered by their plan and those with no health care insurance at all have an incentive to seek assisted suicide/euthanasia so that they do not become a financial burden to their families. Moreover, societal pressures to cut the costs of health care are mounting today. These bring with them a subtle undercurrent in favor of providing assisted suicide and euthanasia to those whose care threatens the integrity of publicly funded forms of health care, such as Medicare and Medicaid.[12]

6. Changing religious and moral sensibilities about suicide

In earlier times, those who committed suicide or attempted to do so were usually condemned by Christians. This is changing today. The involuntary character of many suicides due to what Karl Barth calls "affliction" leads some Christians to conclude that most who attempt suicide are not fully responsible for their act.[13] These Christians no longer view all suicides as sinful turning away from God, but view many as the result of physical, personal, and financial pressures. Such pressures may weigh down without relief so that suicide seems the only escape from affliction. Thus, pity and compassion seem more appropriate responses to those who attempt or commit suicide than judgmental and punitive ones, they believe. Those who take their own lives, they hold, should be entrusted to the mercy of God.

Do these features of contemporary life offer new knowledge or circumstances that compel us to reevaluate traditional Christian guidance on assisted suicide and euthanasia? We struggle to understand how to respond to this difficult question, mindful of our responsibility to recognize fundamental moral principles within our tradition and to exercise our powers of reason and choice in ways that reflect our allegiance in mind and heart to God. ■

B

Key Terms and Distinctions

Before we consider the arguments concerning assisted suicide and euthanasia, it is important to explain what we mean by certain terms and distinctions. It is vital to give "assisted suicide" and "euthanasia" as precise a meaning as we can, for clear definitions are essential to moral discourse.

It is also pastorally important to understand the meaning of these terms and distinctions, for people sometimes mistakenly believe that they are responsible for killing a relative in the medical setting when they have done nothing of the sort. Some reach such distressing conclusions because they have confused removing life-sustaining treatment that has proven useless from a seriously ill person with killing that person. Understanding the meaning of certain key terms and certain moral distinctions will help avert such agonizing misunderstandings.

1. The meaning of assisted suicide and euthanasia
a. Suicide

"Suicide" is the act of intentionally taking one's own life. It can be done for any number of reasons, such as to end one's own pain and suffering, to avoid being a burden to one's family, or to avert financial ruin. Where there is no intention to end one's own life, there is no suicide. Thus, those who risk their lives in order to save someone else or who refuse to renounce their religious beliefs knowing this will mean death do not commit suicide if they die as a result of these actions, for they do not explicitly intend their own deaths.

i. In "assisted suicide," one person intentionally gives another the means to take his or her own life, at the latter's request, often to relieve the person's pain and suffering. For instance, if a husband were to provide his wife, who was terminally ill from cancer and in pain, a large quantity of poison at her request, this would amount to assisted suicide.

ii. In "physician-assisted suicide," a doctor, acting on a patient's request, provides that person with the means to end his or her life, often to relieve the person's pain and suffering. The physician provides the means, but the final act is the patient's. For example, if a physician were to give a patient with a terminal condition who requested it a prescription for a large dose of barbiturates, knowing that the patient would use the medication to commit suicide, this would be physician-assisted suicide.

b. Euthanasia

"Euthanasia" is a term that has not been used consistently. In the original Greek, it meant "a good death." In modern usage however, it has taken on a different, more specific meaning. "Euthanasia" has come to mean that one person intentionally causes the death of another who is terminally or seriously ill, often to end the latter's pain and suffering.[14] Euthanasia requires the explicit intention to end another's life. For instance, if a son were to inject his father, who was in great agony as he was dying, with a lethal dose of a drug in order to end his father's suffering, this would be euthanasia.

We can distinguish several kinds of euthanasia according to whether the person whose life is ended has requested this and had the capacity to make such a request.[15]

i. Thus, in "voluntary euthanasia," a competent, informed person asks another to end his or her life and is not coerced into doing so. For example, if a terminally ill, competent man who was under no compulsion, asked his wife, a nurse, to give him a lethal injection in order in order to end his life, this would amount to voluntary euthanasia.

ii. In "involuntary euthanasia," a person who has the capacity for informed choice, but who has not requested euthanasia, or who has rejected euthanasia, is killed. For example, if a terminally ill man who wished to live as long as possible were given an overdose of a barbiturate without his permission by an attendant who felt sorry for him, this would be involuntary euthanasia.

iii. In "nonvoluntary euthanasia," a person who does not have the capacity for informed choice is killed. For example, if a woman with senile dementia and in great pain and suffering had her life taken by her daughter, this would be non-voluntary euthanasia.

iv. "Passive euthanasia," by which is meant withdrawing or withholding treatment with the result that death follows, is sometimes distinguished from "active euthanasia," by which is meant directly ending life. Using the term "passive euthanasia," however, can create confusion because "euthanasia" today generally refers to bringing about death intentionally. The withholding or withdrawal of treatment that is deemed useless or burdensome, however, need not involve a specific intent to cause death. Doctors realize that patients may well die when treatment is removed, but the fact that they would not act to kill patients should they not die after treatment removal indicates that they do not intend to cause death. [See B. 3. The distinction between stopping treatment and assisted suicide/euthanasia.] To avoid such confusion, we do not employ the terms "passive euthanasia" and "active euthanasia" in this report and instead refer to "withholding or withdrawing treatment" and "euthanasia."

Those who support the introduction of euthanasia generally approve only of voluntary euthanasia, for they consider it morally essential that a person's life be ended only if he or she wishes to have this done and has the capacity to make such a choice. Controversial proposals have been made for nonvoluntary euthanasia of those who cannot give consent because they are mentally incapacitated. Involuntary euthanasia, in contrast, is almost universally condemned.

The conditions under which it is considered moral to provide euthanasia vary among those who support this practice. Some would allow it only for those who are declared terminally ill.

Others would extend it to those who are not dying imminently, but who are incurably ill and in pain and suffering. The *Newark Report*, for instance, does so.[16] Still others would allow euthanasia for those with untreatable mental illness. In the Netherlands, for example, euthanasia has been extended to a person with mental illness, but no physical disorder.[17] Because of the diversity of conditions under which different persons and groups would allow it, we can provide no definition of euthanasia that indicates the conditions under which it necessarily and universally occurs.

c. The distinction between assisted suicide and euthanasia

Some who favor assisted suicide do not support euthanasia. We find these practices very similar in most respects, however. The major difference between the two is in who actually performs the fatal act—the patient or another, perhaps a physician or family member. Some argue that suicide is psychologically more difficult to carry out than euthanasia because a person has to have a hand in his or her own death. Therefore, they say that suicide is more clearly expressive of a person's wishes and this makes it more acceptable morally than euthanasia. While suicide can, but does not necessarily, provide a greater safeguard against an incompetent or erroneous decision for death than euthanasia, if deliberately bringing about death is wrong, then it is wrong whether a person kills him or herself with considerable emotional difficulty or if another does it for that person, making it psychologically easier for him or her. If it is right, then the degree of emotional hardship through which the person goes prior to dying does not make an essential moral difference between them. Consequently, this report does not distinguish between the morality of assisted suicide and euthanasia, and uses the terms in concert.

2. The distinction between providing adequate pain relief to the dying and assisted suicide/euthanasia

It has long been a part of the Christian tradition that it is morally acceptable to provide drugs to relieve pain in the dying, even though this may hasten death. The use of drugs with the explicit purpose of ending their lives, however, is not. The moral difference between these acts rests on at least two factors: (a) the causal impact of the type and amount of drug used and (b) the intent of the caregiver and patient.

a. The significance of the type and amount of drug used

To provide pain relief, the primary action of the drug chosen must be to lessen the perception of pain in those who are conscious. Narcotics (opioids) and other analgesics do this. Consequently, these drugs are routinely prescribed for those who are terminally ill for pain relief. Increased doses of narcotics may be required as terminal illness progresses to control pain in some patients; these doses may hasten their death if they depress respiration. The use of potent narcotics, therefore, requires careful titration and intimate knowledge of the individual's response to the amount of drug given. When appropriate doses of these drugs are given, it is accurate to attribute a death they may hasten to the underlying disease, not to the drugs or to the caregiver. When a dose of narcotics known to be lethal is administered to a patient, however, the death of the patient is attributable to the drugs and the caregiver providing them, and this amounts to euthanasia.

The primary action of barbiturates, in contrast, is not to lessen the perception of pain in those who are conscious, but to provide sedation and loss of consciousness. Barbiturates are well known for their capacity to cause death; they have been used to kill patients intentionally. Other drugs, such as insulin, potassium, and even carbon monoxide have also been implicated in controversies over whether pain relief or assisted suicide/euthanasia have been provided to persons who receive drugs and subsequently die. None of these compounds has as its primary action the relief of pain. Unless some specific medical condition warrants the use of one of these drugs,[18] their pharmacology speaks against almost all intent of those using them other than to cause the death of those receiving them. Consequently, there is a rebuttable presumption that when these drugs are used they are being given to bring about death, and this amounts to euthanasia.

b. The meaning and moral role of intention and foreseen side effects

Clearly, intention plays an important role in judging the morality of our acts. Our intention is what we aim at, our objective in acting. Intentions are significant in the Christian tradition for distinguishing between right and wrong acts. Jesus stressed intent, for instance, when he criticized the Pharisees, saying that they hypocritically concealed their self-aggrandizing intentions behind a mask of piety (Matthew 5:20; 16:6; 21:43; 23:2, 13; Luke 11:39, 42).

It is important morally to distinguish between what we intend and what we foresee might occur as a side effect of our actions, but do not directly intend. The side effect is not the goal of our action, even though we know that it will probably occur. Thus, the surgeon foresees that operating on a patient with prostate cancer will result in post-operative pain, but the surgeon does not perform such surgery *in order to* produce that pain. The surgeon and patient's intent is to prevent the spread of cancer. This justifies the operation and the ensuing pain.

Similarly, the caregiver who provides narcotics in appropriate doses with the intent of relieving the pain of a terminally ill patient foresees that the patient may die sooner as a result. Yet the caregiver does not necessarily give these drugs with the intent to hasten the patient's death. Both caregiver and patient believe that the intent of alleviating pain justifies taking the chance of allowing death to come sooner. For this reason, the General Convention of the church stated in 1994 that:

> Palliative treatment to relieve the pain of persons with progressive incurable illnesses, even if done with the knowledge that a hastened death may result, is consistent with theological tenets regarding the sanctity of life.

Still, even when they are not intended, the side effects of our actions can be morally relevant. Kenneth Kirk, a noted Anglican theologian writing in the 1920s, declared that "We are responsible for the foreseen consequences of our actions as much as for the actions themselves."[19] If so, how can we tell when it is morally justifiable to allow a negative side effect, such as pain from surgery or an earlier death from pain medication, to occur? A foreseeable negative side effect must be evaluated as morally acceptable in light of the main purpose of our action. The value of the intended effect must be sufficiently great that it justifies the possibility that the unintended side effect will occur. When we give drugs to the dying to relieve pain, foreseeing that death may occur sooner, we judge that the moral importance of providing pain relief to the dying is greater than that of averting death for a brief time.

In assessing the morality of such situations, it is difficult to know objectively the intent of those involved. Indeed, it can be difficult to sift out our own intentions from the complex and often conflicting feelings that overwhelm us when we, or those we love, are near death. Yet it is important personally and pastorally to realize that it is not necessarily wrong to desire death for a dying person. We may desire this because it involves an end to pain and suffering or because it is an entry into eternal life. Because we are not the helpless victims of our desires, we can decide against acting on them when this would be wrong; we can choose instead to act from morally right intentions. Our intentions can control our actions in circumstances when they conflict with our desires.[20] Thus, when we give narcotics to the dying, we may, in fact, intend to relieve pain, not to bring about death— even though we may desire that the person die. We may pray for death for the person and yet not act with the intention of killing him or her.

c. Summary, criticism, and response

In summary, a basic difference between providing adequate pain relief and assisted suicide/euthanasia is that in the former, death may be inadvertently hastened, whereas in assisted suicide/euthanasia, death is intentionally brought about. "There is a clear distinction to be drawn between rendering someone unconscious at the risk of killing him and killing him in order to render him unconscious," a 1975 Anglican Working Group observed.[21] It is morally and practically essential to distinguish between providing adequate pain relief and assisted suicide/euthanasia in this way. Otherwise, physicians will be reluctant to provide adequate pain relief to dying patients because they fear being viewed as killers.

Some critics of this view of the significance of intentions maintain that since the results can be the same in both acts—a patient dies—it is meaningless to distinguish between providing adequate pain relief and assisted suicide/euthanasia on the basis of intentions. [See Appendix 1. Two Recent Federal Courts of Appeals Decisions.] They contend that the distinction between what we intend and what we foresee denies the fact that when dying patients are offered a pain-relieving drug that hastens their death, the drug causes their death. Moreover, in their view, the false distinction conceals the reality in such instances that the death is intended.

That death is not necessarily caused by drugs and is not necessarily intended when pain-relieving drugs hasten death is exhibited by the discussion above. It is also exhibited by the fact that it is possible that the administration of pain-relieving drugs can *lengthen*, rather than shorten the lives of terminally ill patients. This is because these drugs help them to reduce stress responses, become less depressed, and more likely to accept food and fluids. If the intention of doctors were to kill their terminally ill patients, they would not provide these pain-relieving drugs knowing that they might extend the lives of these patients. They would instead give these patients drugs that would surely end their lives.

3. The distinction between withholding and withdrawing treatment and assisted suicide/euthanasia

A distinction must also be drawn between withholding and withdrawing treatment for a terminally ill person, thereby allowing him or her to die, and assisted suicide/euthanasia.

a. The distinction stated

When doctors and patients agree to end treatment that is no longer effective or beneficial, they stop a medical battle that cannot be won and allow death to come. For example, they may conclude that intensive care for a critically ill patient with multiple organ failure can no longer offer him a chance of recovery. It is morally acceptable to refuse or withdraw treatment when it (1) does not provide a reasonable hope of success in sustaining life or restoring health or (2) results in an undue burden on the patient. When this is the case, doctors may regretfully ask permission to remove all forms of medical technology keeping the patient alive. This does not mean that doctors and patients or their surrogates choose death in such circumstances. Instead, they choose to end certain treatments that are no longer helpful. Patients or their surrogates have a legal and moral right to refuse treatment in such circumstances.

When assisted suicide or euthanasia are carried out, in contrast, doctors or patients intentionally perform an act, such as injecting a lethal dose of barbiturates, for the purpose of bringing about death. They do not end useless treatment, but directly end a life. The authors of *On Dying Well* observed that:

> euthanasia implies killing, and it is misleading to extend it to cover decisions not to preserve life by artificial means when it would be better for the patient to be allowed to die. Such decisions, coupled with a determination to give the patient as good a death as possible, may be quite legitimate.[22]

b. Criticism and response

Some argue here, as they did in discussing pain relief, that since the outcome can be the same in both withholding and withdrawing treatment and assisted suicide/euthanasia—a person ends up dead—there is no moral difference between them. [See Appendix 1. Two Recent Federal Courts of Appeals Decisions.] In both cases, they argue, the death of the patient is caused by the way that medical technology is used, not by the disease. Moreover, an intention to end the patient's life is involved in both cases, they maintain. On this view, the intentions of those acting are identical in both instances and therefore cannot provide a distinguishing moral consideration. It is the consequences that count.

This argument overlooks the vastly different contexts in which these acts are carried out. When physicians remove the barrier they have erected against death for a patient, they do not cause an ensuing death, but open the possibility that it will come. It may not come, as the case of Karen Quinlan, who lived for almost a decade after the removal of her respirator, attests. Yet, some respond, we would say that a malicious relative who removes a respirator from a terminally ill patient causes his death. Therefore, they maintain, to be consistent we must also say that physicians who remove respirators from terminally ill patients also cause their death.[23]

This seems inaccurate. Because the malicious relative's act is terribly wrong, we tend to think of it as causing death. But what he does is to allow the patient to die; he does not cause his death. It is the underlying disease that does this. Indeed, he might well be ready to act more directly to cause death should the patient fail to die. When doctors remove respirators with patient or surrogate permission, in contrast, they rightly allow the patient to die. They are not prepared to smother the patient should he or she remain alive. To further illustrate this point about causality in respirator removal, consider the case in which a man slowly poisons his wife over a period of several years and she ends up in an intensive care unit in hopeless condition. When the doctor removes the respirator with permission from an appropriate surrogate, the physician does not kill the wife. It is the husband who causes her death, for he has brought about her underlying condition.

Situations in which treatment is useless or too burdensome *morally warrant* the withdrawal of a respirator. It is morally appropriate to remove a respirator when it cannot achieve the goal for which it was begun—to reverse the patient's downhill course toward death—or because it is too burdensome to the patient. The context of giving a lethal drug is quite different. In this situation, treatment is not necessarily useless or overly burdensome to the patient. In this context, those who act do so in order to induce death. Whether this is morally warranted is not built into the context, but is the question at issue here. As distinct from the withdrawal of treatment context, death in such situations is not a side effect of a morally warranted act, but is the direct result of the intentional use of medical measures—a use whose moral acceptability is open to debate.

The outcome of the acts performed in each context, consequently, is not the only factor to consider when assessing the moral difference between withdrawing treatment and allowing a patient to die and directly ending that patient's life. The morality of these two kinds of situations differs because they present different sorts of causal contexts and are generally done with different intentions. Moreover, one is clearly warranted morally, whereas the morality of the other is the subject of considerable debate. ■

C

Views about Ending and Extending Life in the Christian Tradition

The Jewish and Christian traditions have valued human life and prohibited taking it without a just cause. Intentionally to end our own life or deliberately to kill another is considered seriously wrong within the Christian tradition except in self-defense, war, and often in capital punishment. At the same time, that tradition has not viewed life as an absolute good that must be extended for as long as possible. Life may be sacrificed in the defense of others or, as in the case of martyrdom, in telling the truth about one's faith. A closer look at views of suicide, euthanasia, and the extension of life that have been held over the course of the Christian tradition will explain these claims more specifically.

1. Suicide in the Christian tradition
a. Scriptural references
The Christian tradition has from early times consistently and unequivocally prohibited suicide, the intentional taking of one's own life. The scriptural roots of this prohibition are in the horror of shedding innocent blood attested in the story of Cain and Abel and throughout scripture, most notably in the Sixth Commandment (Exodus 20:13). The Christian tradition has almost universally interpreted the commandment against murder to apply to taking one's own life.

The moral status of suicide does not arise as a specific topic in scripture. In the few accounts of suicide in the Bible, it is, for the most part, committed by figures whose actions have brought them to a final act of despair or who have wished to avoid shame and dishonor. Ahitopel hanged himself after David's son failed to take his advice in his rebellion against his father (2 Samuel 17:23). Abimelech, who was mortally wounded by a woman in battle, ordered his armor-bearer to kill him to save him from public disgrace (Judges 9:50-66). Saul was wounded in battle and committed suicide to spare himself mockery by a victorious enemy (1 Samuel 31:1-6; 2 Samuel 15:1; 1 Chronicles 10:1-13). Zimri set a house afire and burned himself to death when he was about to be captured after having wrongfully killed the king of Israel and all his house (1 Kings 16:18-19). The warrior, Razis, killed himself rather than suffer dishonor (2 Maccabees 14:41-6). Judas hanged himself after betraying Christ (Matthew 27:5). Paul, on the other hand, prevented his jailer from committing suicide (Acts 16:27-28). The silence of scripture on the moral status of suicide cannot be counted as approval of or indifference to the practice. Indeed, it can be concluded from the fact that suicide occurs only rarely and without endorsement that it was not approved in scripture.

Christians, such as Paul, viewed their own acceptance of suffering and death as a sharing in, or even completion of, Christ's sufferings (see Colossians 1:24, 2 Corinthians 1:5). They ardently opposed self-inflicted death out of suffering or despair. Indeed, there is no evidence of any Christian committing suicide for any reason in the first 250 years of the Christian era.[24]

b. Earlier Christian views

Some Christians took to flaunting their faith as a way of courting their own martyrdom. This came to be frowned upon, and the church accepted a position enunciated by Clement of Alexandria (ca. 155-ca. 220) that honored martyrdom, but stressed the importance of doing all one could, short of betraying one's faith, to avoid it. A succession of church leaders took a strong stand against suicide. Augustine (354-430) denounced it in the *City of God* as a cowardly way of escaping the pain and suffering of this life. Aquinas (1225-1274) expressed classical objections to suicide, arguing that it was absolutely prohibited because 1) it violates our natural self-love and inclination to preserve our being, 2) it offends the human community, of which each human being is a part, and 3) it offends God, who offers life as a gift.

c. Later Christian views

The traditional Christian opposition to suicide became rooted in law. Prohibitions against burying those who had committed suicide in consecrated ground can be traced back to the sixth century. Such persons in most Christian countries were declared felons after their death and often had their property confiscated. Clergy in the Church of England were prohibited by rubric from saying the Burial Office over those who had laid violent hands on themselves. Anglicans have since abandoned this prohibition in this century.

By the sixteenth century, some Christians explicitly discussed suicide and euthanasia in the face of illness.[25] In an imaginary land named Utopia depicted by Thomas More (1478-1535), a Roman Catholic, suicide and euthanasia were encouraged for those suffering from incurable diseases accompanied by continuous pain. Speculation that the book provides satire, rather than a serious argument for suicide and euthanasia is supported by the fact that as More awaited his own execution in the Tower of London, he wrote *A Dialogue of Comfort: Against Tribulation*, in which he argued against these acts. John Donne (1572-1631), the English poet and Anglican divine, wrote the first defense of suicide in English in *Biathanatos*. There he defined suicide very broadly to include all cases of willing death, including Christ's death on the cross. Donne did not permit suicide undertaken for self-interest, however. The work is difficult to interpret, and some hypothesize that he did not mean to defend suicide in the sense in which it has been defined in this document.

Anglicans, sharing the Christian theological consensus, took for granted the prohibition of suicide. Cranmer's Catechism was typical in its condemnation of the suicide. Jeremy Taylor (1613-67) in *Ductor Dubitantium or the Rule of Conscience*, condemned suicide as "impiety and rebellion against God; it is desertion of our military station, and a violation of the proprieties and peculiar rights of God... It is against the law, and the voice, and the very prime inclination of Nature. Every thing will preserve itself." Only recently have some Anglicans, such as Hastings Rashdall,[26] W.R. Inge,[27] and Joseph Fletcher,[28] maintained that suicide might be permissible to end extreme and incurable physical suffering.

In short, over the course of its history, with few exceptions, the Christian tradition has condemned suicide. Even when faced with terrible forms of torture and martyrdom, Christians have maintained that it would be wrong to attempt self-killing. Suicide is a statement that there is no reason to continue living. It is often argued that to make this judgment and take our own lives is to reject God's purposes for us.

2. Euthanasia in the Christian tradition
a. Scriptural references

According to the Hebrew tradition, those who kill the sick in order to spare them from pain are to be viewed as murderers. There has been a widespread conviction among Christians, as well, that the Sixth Commandment, which Jesus reaffirmed, forbids euthanasia.[29]

Paul, when faced with what has generally been taken as an unspecified physical ailment, expressed a desire to die, but went on living, accepting his affliction as necessary for God's purposes (2 Corinthians 5:1-10; 12:8-9). In the face of severe and inexorable pain caused by persecution and even torture, he and others taught that Christians were to remain steadfast and patient, but were not to kill one another.

b. Earlier Christian views

Like Paul, the early Christians did not counsel the faithful to escape pain and suffering by asking others to kill them. The Church of the second century rejected the view that Christ had abrogated the Sixth Commandment against murder along with other parts of Jewish law. The Ten Commandments, Irenaeus declared, were fully revealed by Jesus and are God's permanent will for human beings. The rejection of killing, coupled with the acceptance of physical suffering, was clearly maintained from the early church through Augustine.

The prohibition against killing innocent persons (those not guilty of committing a serious crime or deliberately threatening the life of others) continued into the later church. Aquinas was deeply impressed by the view of the Jewish scholar Maimonides that killing an innocent person, "whether he is healthy or about to die from natural causes," is wrong. Euthanasia for those in pain and suffering, Aquinas maintained, was contrary to Christian tradition, natural law, and the well-being of society. It violated the dominion of God over human life. Aquinas spelled out in some detail the Christian position that the only justification for taking the life of another is to protect innocent life. Three circumstances in which killing may be allowed are (1) self-defense, (2) the defense of the innocent from an unjust aggressor in war, and (3) the defense of society in the case of capital punishment. The purpose of killing in these instances is to preserve one's own or another's life against an unjust attack. Killing is acceptable in these circumstances only if it is necessary to overcome the evil being addressed.[30]

c. Later Christian views

Early Protestantism grew in a crucible of suffering due to war, political turmoil, plague, and other diseases. Neither Luther, who endured great physical suffering due to a constellation of medical conditions, nor Calvin, who was in fragile health, approved of euthanasia as a means of ending the misery brought on by illness. Both viewed sickness as an opportunity for gaining increased confidence in God's presence and power, and thus bringing about spiritual healing.

In the *ars moriendi*, or art of dying literature, the recommendation to those caring for the dying was to provide ease and comfort, rather than to cause their death. Works such as *The Rule and Exercise of Holy Dying* by Anglican divine Jeremy Taylor explained the importance of preparing for death, and maintained that we should not choose our cause of death.

Euthanasia has had few advocates within the Christian tradition. Within the Anglican tradition, Fletcher was its strongest proponent. He argued on the basis of biblical and humanistic notions of mercy, love, and dignity that the ending of human life is justified when it is demoralized by terminal disease.[31] In contrast, David H. Smith has summarized the view of the Anglican tradition that assisted suicide/euthanasia represent:

> a desertion or betrayal of others and an impatient assertion of the self against conditions of finitude that are part of embodied existence... From the Anglican viewpoint the individualism that voluntary euthanasia represents is

a mistaken interpretation of reality. The mistake, moreover, is not strictly intellectual, for in a real community
conventions must nurture care and trust. Proposals to
legalize voluntary euthanasia are fundamentally pitiless.[32]

This approach to euthanasia was taken in a resolution adopted at
the 1991 General Convention of the Episcopal Church and reaffirmed at the 1994 General Convention. The resolution stated:

> [I]t is morally wrong and unacceptable to intentionally
> take a human life in order to relieve the suffering caused
> by incurable illness. This would include the intentional
> shortening of another person's life by the use of a lethal
> dose of medication or poison, the use of lethal weapons,
> homicidal acts, and other forms of active euthanasia.

3. Extending life and the sanctity of life in the Christian tradition

Are Christians obliged to keep people alive as long as possible by
means of medical technology? The term "sanctity of life" has
been used to convey the enormous value that God ascribes to our
lives. We are made in God's own image and likeness, "a little
lower than the angels, and crowned with glory and honor" (Psalm
8:5). We reflect the image of God in our capacities to love and to
rejoice in our own being, as well as in our ability to make reasoned, responsible choices. Moreover, each of us is infinitely precious to God. Christians have responded to the claims of God's
love by cherishing earthly life.

Some Christians hold that the value God ascribes to human
life makes it so sacred that it must be preserved as long as possible. They believe that whether it is comatose life, severely
impaired life, or suffering life, we are obliged to use all techniques
available to maintain human life. Not to do so is wrong because
it gives us a power over life and death that belongs to God. This
position has been termed "vitalism" because it takes biological life
as an ultimate value.

However, the central Christian tradition holds that while biological life is a fundamental good, it is not an absolute good.

There are values that are weightier than that of life. We are called to risk—not take—our lives at times for the sake of God and others. Christ implicitly indicated this when he observed that the good shepherd lays down his life for the sheep (John 10:10) and that there is no greater love than to give up one's life for a friend (John 15:13). Life, for Christ, is an extremely high value, but certain other values—love of God and others—are even weightier. His own death revealed this. Saints and martyrs throughout the history of the church have given up their lives for the sake of higher values embodied in their faith. They have not chosen death, but have been ready to accept it. The concept of the sanctity of life, therefore, means that human life is precious and to be respected and protected, but it also recognizes that life can be risked for the sake of values and duties that are even more significant.

Nothing in the central Christian tradition requires us to extend our lives for as long as possible, even though they are valuable. Indeed, "when one considers all the highly sophisticated systems and techniques of modern medicine, it is frightening to envisage the possible consequences of a strict adherence to such a rule."[33] While there is a Christian presumption that we have a duty to nurture and preserve our lives, this presumption may be overcome when medical techniques 1) do not offer us a reasonable hope of success and/or 2) cannot be used without excessive pain, cost, or other serious burden. Thus, when treatment would be useless or overwhelmingly burdensome, it is morally acceptable within the Christian tradition to withdraw it and allow a person to die.[34]

Christians, while called by God to life, have reason not to fear death. We see death as that occasion when the love and power of God in Christ will break forth in its fullness. The meaning that Christians find in death is not the nothingness of final extinction, but the complete revelation of the being and love of God. Death is the gate to eternal life. Therefore, we need not dread death and need not do everything humanly possible to keep it at bay. Our faith calls us to trust in God and the promises of Christ near the end of our lives. ■

D

Brief Summaries of Arguments for Accepting and for Rejecting Assisted Suicide/Euthanasia

We present here in brief major arguments for accepting and for rejecting assisted suicide/euthanasia that have been used by Christians. These summaries are meant to provide readers with an initial impression of the scope and import of the arguments of those who favor and who oppose assisted suicide/euthanasia. While this runs the danger of overemphasizing the differences between them, rather than identifying common ground, it is necessary to understand the fullness of the vision of each side before mutual understanding can occur.

We have chosen to present the set of arguments for accepting and for rejecting these practices separately, rather than pair off each side on specific points. While viewing the opposing arguments in dialogue on particular issues would offer readers a sense of which side is stronger on each of them, it would not provide them with a sense of the overall strength of each set. Moreover, to arrange the arguments according to the issues they address would necessarily weaken one side, for each side differs about which issues are most important and should be addressed first. Readers should note that after the more extended discussion of each set of arguments in the next section, we present other perspectives that cannot readily be categorized as for or against assisted suicide/euthanasia. [See G. Arguments for Justifying or Excusing Assisted Suicide/Euthanasia in Rare, Extreme Circumstances.]

1. **Brief summary of religious (and related) arguments**
   for accepting **assisted suicide/euthanasia**
   a. **Respect for autonomy or self-determination calls**
      for allowing assisted suicide/euthanasia
   Because we are self-determining agents created in the image of

God to make our own choices, we have a right and responsibility to choose whether to end our lives by means of assisted suicide/euthanasia, some claim. When we can no longer serve God or others by remaining alive, they hold, it is not wrong to exercise our freedom of choice to bring about our own death or to ask others to do this.

b. God's purposes and sovereignty would still be honored if assisted suicide/euthanasia were allowed

As we allow certain exceptions to the rule against killing in wartime and in self-defense, so should we also allow euthanasia as an exception, it is argued by some who favor assisted suicide/euthanasia. Those who are critically ill and suffering severely should have their ordeal ended by taking their lives directly, on this view. Some have claimed that the willful destruction of human life can be justified when the good sought outweighs the evil of the act. Thus, they maintain that killing a seriously ill person can be a morally creative act that achieves greater good in a person's life taken as a whole.

c. Assisted suicide/euthanasia are an appropriate moral response to pain and suffering

Our inherent dignity is violated when we are forced to endure pain and suffering due to the overuse of medical treatment at the end of life, some argue. Our suffering is validated and to be endured only when it is for the sake of Christ. God's purposes are not to force us to endure unredemptive suffering, but to relieve such suffering and to lead us into life in God. Assisted suicide/euthanasia provide a compassionate way of ending unredemptive suffering.

d. To curb the unrelenting power of medical technology we must use assisted suicide/euthanasia

Some who would accept assisted suicide/euthanasia claim that technology has taken control of the process of dying, making it impossible for us to die naturally. Therefore, they say, we must reestablish a measure of control over dying by providing assisted suicide/euthanasia to those voluntarily requesting these options.

e. An analogy with the rightness of decisions to with draw treatment supports assisted suicide/euthanasia

It is morally acceptable to withdraw treatment and allow patients to die. Yet those who have no need to be maintained by life-sustaining technology, some argue, have no way to die quickly. Instead, they are at risk of going through an extended and agonizing period of dying. Since there is no real distinction between killing and letting die, this argument continues, we should provide them with assisted suicide/euthanasia so that they, too, can die quickly and painlessly.

f. Physicians appropriately participate in assisted suicide/euthanasia

When healing is no longer possible, some who support assisted suicide/euthanasia maintain, physicians can honor their duty to provide comfort to patients by assisting them to die quickly by means of assisted suicide/euthanasia. Physicians are uniquely qualified for this role, those holding this position say, by their professional training.

g. The dangers of assisted suicide/euthanasia to the community can be overcome

While abuses of assisted suicide/euthanasia might occur were these practices allowed, some argue, their involuntary use and misuse can be avoided by careful regulation.

h. Precautions can be taken against financial coercion of the critically ill into assisted suicide/euthanasia

It is essential to enact safeguards against the financial coercion of critically ill people into assisted suicide/euthanasia by self-interested relatives or a cost-conscious health care system, those who would promote assisted suicide/euthanasia acknowledge.

2. Brief summary of religious (and related) arguments *for* *rejecting* assisted suicide/euthanasia

a. God's purposes would be impeded and God's sover eignty violated if assisted suicide/euthanasia were condoned

We are not our own, but hold our lives in trust for God. God has created each of us for a purpose. It is God to whom we are accountable for how we live—and how we die. We violate God's sovereignty and intrude on God's purposes, some maintain, when we deliberately end our lives. Moreover, we are created to live in community with one another, caring for one another and working to achieve the common good. Self-killing would necessarily diminish our bonds with others, they argue, for it would introduce socially-sanctioned killing of the innocent into society and would cut out of human fellowship those most in need of it.

b. Some pain and suffering is inevitable; we are called to alleviate it through morally acceptable means, rather than by killing

Suffering is an inevitable consequence of our finite human condition. It can sanctify and transform us, bringing us closer to God. This does not mean that we must bear all suffering that befalls us. We are called to alleviate pain and suffering when we can do so by morally acceptable means. Instances in which the seriously ill experience pain and suffering could be avoided, those opposed to assisted suicide/euthanasia maintain, if currently available palliative care measures were adequately employed.

c. Christian moral constraints on autonomy work against allowing assisted suicide/ euthanasia

The sheer fact that a choice for death is ours does not make it right. We are asked by God to use our freedom of choice in ways that accord with Christian values and virtues. Acts that would deliberately end innocent human lives, even at the request of those to be killed, some argue, deny God's purposes and violate the integrity of the community that is the body of Christ.

d. The availability of assisted suicide/euthanasia would eliminate our choice to remain alive without having to justify our existence

If assisted suicide/euthanasia were available, our choice to remain alive without having to explain this choice to others would be jeopardized, it has been argued. Instead, we would be called to give an account to others for our decision to continue living. The availability of assisted suicide/euthanasia would bring pressure on us to end our lives or else justify our decision not to do so, some maintain. Consequently, they say, we could no longer receive life as a given.

e. Appropriate treatment of pain and suffering would decrease requests for assisted suicide/euthanasia

Persons in severe pain want to get rid of their pain, studies show, not to be put to death. The efforts of the medical profession to relieve pain and suffering, however, are sadly deficient on the whole and require major improvement. Experts in pain management state that the pain of those who are terminally ill can be controlled by developing an individualized plan with each patient to provide pain relief and comfort care using available medical, anesthetic, surgical, and psychological approaches. Assisted suicide/euthanasia, some therefore claim, are not needed to end pain and suffering.

f. The role of the physician is to heal, not to kill

Taking human life is contrary to the calling of medicine, which focuses on healing. Some argue that to combine killing with healing in acts of assisted suicide/euthanasia would undermine patient trust in physicians and corrupt the very meaning of medicine.

g. Other means can be used to respond to the overuse of medical technology than assisted suicide/euthanasia

Assisted suicide/euthanasia represent an unnecessary "technological fix" for current dilemmas created by the overuse of medical technology, some who oppose these practices hold. Rather than kill patients to avoid technologically-sustained dying, they say, patients can refuse treatment through advance directives. Moreover, caregivers can employ innovative approaches to the care of the dying offered by hospice and can improve the integration of palliative care into general medical practice.

h. Assisted suicide/euthanasia present individuals and society with dangers of abuse

Assisted suicide/euthanasia would not be limited to those who are clearly dying, it has been claimed, but would soon be expanded to include those who are chronically ill, have senile dementia, or psychiatric illness. This is occurring in the Netherlands, they maintain. The Dutch experience, these opponents believe, exhibits that once we cross the vital line between allowing to die and killing, the limits suggested in current proposals for assisted suicide/euthanasia will vanish.

i. Persons would be pressured to end their lives for financial reasons if assisted suicide/euthanasia were available

In the current climate of health care cost-cutting and profit-taking, some state, assisted suicide/euthanasia provide cheaper alternatives than either comfort care for the dying or aggressive treatment for the incurable. Current efforts to pare down costs create subtle pressures on these patients to kill themselves. Opponents hold that we should not condone a practice that would pressure individuals into ending their lives because they cannot afford to live or because others would benefit financially from their earlier death.

j. The social isolation of the dying, as well as the elderly and some who are disabled, may lead them inappropriately to choose assisted suicide/euthanasia

Dying, in some settings, can be an alienating and isolating experience. When the relational bonds of the seriously ill, elderly, or disabled are disrupted, they may elect assisted suicide/euthanasia out of despair, some aver. Rather than kill the dying, they argue, we should offer them care, compassion, and companionship. ■

E

Arguments for Accepting Assisted Suicide/Euthanasia

Those who favor assisted suicide/euthanasia tend to make two basic claims: 1) we have an obligation to respect individual choice and 2) we have an obligation to relieve suffering, even if this means ending human life. Other considerations, such as our loss of control over dying and the claim that there is no real moral distinction between killing and letting die, as well as the need to regulate socially-approved killing also figure in these arguments.

1. Human choice
a. Respect for autonomy or self-determination calls for allowing assisted suicide/euthanasia

The principle of respect for autonomy recognizes the right of adults to make important decisions about their lives according to their conception of a good life. "A central aspect of human dignity," Dan Brock, a philosopher, says "lies in people's capacity to direct their lives..."[35] In exercising autonomy, people take responsibility for their lives and for the persons they become. The principle of respect for autonomy can be extended, some secular thinkers maintain, to cover decisions people make to end their own lives by assisted suicide/euthanasia.

Christians have distinctive and compelling reasons for taking these claims of autonomy with great seriousness. We are created in the image and likeness of God (Genesis 1:26-27). An essential part of that image is our ability to make free choices. Hans Küng, a Roman Catholic, observes that "life is... a human task and thus made our responsibility... [God] wants to have human beings, in his image, as free, responsible partners."[36] Because we are self-determining agents created to make our own choices, some Christians maintain, we have a right to choose whether to end our lives by means of assisted suicide/euthanasia. They hold that when we can no longer serve God or others by remaining alive and are in great pain and suffering near death, we can freely choose to bring about our own death.

The importance of self-determination or autonomy is emphasized in the *Newark Report*, which maintains it would be right to allow assisted death when "[t]he decision to hasten death is a truly informed and voluntary choice free from external coercion."[37] To this, the report adds a related criterion that "[t]he plan for voluntary assisted death places maximum autonomy and command of the process in the hands of the dying person." It holds that patients need not choose assisted suicide, but they should be allowed the freedom to do so when this seems appropriate to them. The *Newark Report* states:

> We believe that there are cases and circumstances where involuntary prolonged biological existence is a less ethical alternative than a conscientiously chosen and merciful termination of earthly life. In such an exceptional environment, voluntary assisted death may indeed be part of the healing process because it enables the person to die well.[38]

Yet autonomy for the Christian is not unbounded. The *Newark Report*, for instance, does not allow patients to choose death whenever they wish. We can only elect assisted suicide, according to that report, when our condition is either terminal or incurable, the pain and/or suffering are persistent and progressive, and all other reasonable means of amelioration have been exhausted. We cannot simply make an autonomous decision for assisted death and expect others to carry out our wishes, according to the *Newark Report*.

2. God's purposes
a. God's purposes and sovereignty would still be honored if assisted suicide/euthanasia were allowed

Many Christians allow exceptions to the Sixth Commandment which prohibits killing. Joseph Fletcher argues that if we accept killing in wartime and capital punishment as such exceptions, which most Christian do, we should also accept euthanasia as an exception.[39] He goes on to maintain that it is incorrect to translate the Sixth Commandment as "Thou shalt not kill." Instead, it should be rendered as in the responsive decalogue of the *Book of Common Prayer,* "Thou shalt do no murder." Murder involves wrongful killing. To end the lives of those who are sick and suffering, however, is not a form of wrongful killing. Therefore, to perform such acts would not violate the Sixth Commandment, he concludes.

The doctrine of creation, the *Newark Report* holds, means that some destruction of life is inevitable within creation, since "life can be sustained only at the expense of other life." Even so, that report notes, we are required out of reverence for God's creation to avoid the unnecessary destruction of life. "The willful taking of life, however, can be morally justified only if the good desired outweighs the potential evil and only if that good cannot be achieved in a less destructive manner."[40] Thus, in those situations when killing would bring about a balance of good over evil, it can be justified by its good consequences, that report concludes.

The *Newark Report,* in a distinctive interpretation of the 1975 Anglican report, *On Dying Well,* finds that it states that it could be a "morally creative act" to kill a dying person who feels "himself a burden to others as well as to himself." This is because "the greater value could be achieved in a person's life, *taken as a whole,* if he knew that at a certain stage of his dying he would be painlessly put to death rather than be allowed to linger on."[41] Consequently, the *Newark Report* argues that we do not intrude on God's purposes and prevent the realization of God's intentions for our lives when we make intelligent, voluntary decisions to end them in light of the good results this would entail.

b. Assisted suicide/euthanasia are appropriate moral responses to pain and suffering

Because human beings are created in the image of God, we have an inherent dignity. This is violated, those who favor assisted suicide/euthanasia maintain, when we are forced to go through an agonizing period of pain and suffering before our lives end. Hastings Rashdall, an early twentieth century Anglican thinker who condemned suicide in the vast number of cases, suggested that it might be morally acceptable in some extreme cases of pain and suffering.

> There are times when life seems to have lost its value from an intellectual and a moral point of view as well as from a hedonistic one. When life has reduced itself to a slow and painful process of dying, why, it may be thought, should we prolong a useless agony which seems to be as incompatible with moral effort as with enjoyment of life?[42]

Our dignity is assaulted, not only by physical pain, but by the depersonalization associated with prolonged use of life-sustaining technology, loss of control over our bodily functions, and the deterioration of our health, some advocates of assisted suicide/euthanasia hold. Such diminishment serves no discernible spiritual or other purpose, they find. Indeed, they believe it can be destructive of moral and spiritual values and the very dignity with which God has endowed us. It can amount to "radical suffering," which has been defined by Wendy Farley as suffering which "is destructive of the human spirit and cannot be understood as something deserved."[43] We cannot square radical suffering with the will or intention of a loving and just God, she says. Dean Inge once wrote in a similar vein,

> I confess that in this instance I cannot resist the arguments for a modification of the traditional Christian law, which absolutely prohibits suicide in all circumstances. I do not think we can assume that God willed the prolongation of torture for the benefit of the soul of the sufferer."[44]

God's will for humanity is to alleviate suffering, the *Newark Report* observes. God's saving action in Exodus, and again in the life of Jesus, is expressed "in the drawing of humanity from the bondage of suffering into the deeper, creative significance of life in God."[45] That report goes on to declare that Biblical passages where St. Paul rejoices in the virtue of suffering and the abundance of grace that flows through it for the Christian do not glorify suffering for its own sake. Instead, these passages validate suffering *only when* it is for the sake of Christ, according to the *Newark Report*.

St. Paul declared that "suffering produces endurance, and endurance produces character, and character produces hope, and hope does not disappoint us, because God's love has been poured into our hearts by the Holy Spirit that has been given to us" (Romans 5:3-5). In this passage, the Greek term for "suffering" is usually taken to refer to trouble that the Christian may encounter in a godless world, not physical pain. The *Newark Report* states:

> Unless an individual somehow understands suffering due to serious illness as a direct consequence of one's faithful response to the Gospel, endurance of such suffering cannot be seen as a mandate, either moral or theological, on the basis of the scriptural witness. It is not a moral failing to view such suffering as devoid of purpose, and thus without redemptive value. This, coupled with the clear precedent of Jesus' countless efforts to alleviate suffering through his healing ministry, makes clear that there is no obligation incumbent upon the Christian to endure suffering for its own sake.[46]

While the authors of the *Newark Report* do not wish to diminish the sense of purpose of those who experience suffering as an opportunity to deepen their faith, they do not believe that we are required to "suffer virtuously and without release." Assisted suicide provides a way of ending the unredemptive suffering of those who do not elect to undergo it, according to that report.

The Christian tradition teaches that the whole sum and purpose of our existence is to respond to God's call to a loving relationship. Joseph Fletcher, in particular, stresses love as the only basis for Christian moral decisions. "Everything else without exception, all laws and rules and principles and ideals and norms, are only contingent, only valid if they happen to serve love in any situation."[47] Love, he maintains, requires that Christians offer assisted suicide/euthanasia to those who experience pain and suffering as they die. If there is any outstanding provision in the divine law or revealed will of God found in the Bible, it is in the fifth beatitude calling for mercy, Fletcher observes. "The beatitude Blessed are the merciful, for they shall obtain mercy' is still in the New Testament as part of the divine law." We must act from the motive of compassion, which, according to the theology of Atonement, lies behind the crucifixion of Jesus, Fletcher argues.[48] To end the life of a person who is in pain may represent the most loving and compassionate way of caring for him or her.

3. The impact of contemporary medicine

a. To curb the unrelenting power of medical technology we must use assisted suicide/euthanasia

We have lost control over when and how we die. The contemporary explosion of medical technology and sophisticated medical techniques has made it increasingly hard for people to die relatively quickly as they did in the past, some who favor assisted suicide/euthanasia claim. Today they die of degenerative diseases, which often can involve long periods of terminal illness. Many of us fear that our deaths will be preceded by the overzealous employment of technological "miracles" that will keep us alive too long. Indeed, we have become as afraid of dying as we are of death.

"The values of yesterday are colliding with the technological and medical expertise of today," Bishop John S. Spong has declared, "rendering the conclusions of the past inoperative for the future."[49] Joseph Fletcher observed, "To prolong life uselessly, while the personal qualities of freedom, knowledge, self-possession and control, and responsibility are sacrificed is to attack the moral status of a person."[50] Accepting assisted suicide/euthanasia would return a measure of control over the dying process, those who argue along similar lines declare. These forms of ending life represent a final expression of self-control over technology in a death-denying culture that would use all available technological means to keep people alive.

b. An analogy with the rightness of decisions to withdraw treatment supports assisted suicide/euthanasia

Patients and physicians are under no obligation to prolong life through the use of treatments that are disproportionately burdensome. [See C. 3. Extending life and the sanctity of life in the

Christian tradition.] If a medical treatment does not reverse a patient's course toward death and only prolongs suffering with no hope of cure, it may be withdrawn or withheld. Today a significant proportion of deaths in the United States occur after a decision has been made to withdraw medical interventions. However, patients who do not require treatment with medical technology may take longer to die, often with greater physical suffering. This is difficult to justify, some claim.

An example presented by an author of the *Newark Report* is one in which two terminally ill people with the same condition, such as pancreatic cancer, both face a difficult period of dying.[51] Should one suffer respiratory arrest, he could be put on a ventilator, which then could be withdrawn, allowing him to die. Another might not be fortunate enough to arrest. He would continue to live, experiencing pain and suffering until he dies. There is a lack of equity, this author finds, between the way that these two patients are treated that could be remedied if assisted suicide were made available to the second.

Further, some believe that when life-sustaining treatment is withdrawn, dying can be agonizingly slow and unpredictable in some instances. Patients and those close to them may have to wait anxiously for long periods of time for death to ensue. It is pointless, some who favor assisted suicide/euthanasia hold, to force those in the shadow of death to go through such an extended and tortuous period of dying. Since there is no real moral distinction between killing and letting die, they claim, and we already allow death to be preceded by decisions to withdraw or withhold treatment, we should go one step further and allow death to be preceded by decisions to end life directly.[52] This, they believe, would allow those who want to die to do so quickly, painlessly, and mercifully.

c. Physicians appropriately participate in assisted suicide/euthanasia

When healing is no longer possible, physicians have a duty to provide comfort and care to their patients. Honorable, dedicated, and compassionate physicians today are recognizing this duty, some claim, by actively aiding terminally ill patients who wish to die. Many carry out assisted suicide/euthanasia in secret to avoid legal complications, it has been averred.[53]

Providing this service does not threaten their professional integrity, those who support doing so claim, but instead allows health care professionals to provide good medical care to those at the end of life.[54] Moreover, patients' trust of their physicians would increase, rather than diminish, they maintain, if they were assured that doctors would provide them with assisted suicide or euthanasia when they requested them.

Several considerations are used to argue in favor of having physicians carry out this task. First, physicians can establish how serious an illness is and can certify that all available forms of treatment and pain relief have been exhausted. Second, physicians are qualified to prescribe or provide drugs to patients, for they know what dosage will cause death and are less likely to create botched attempts. Moreover, only physicians can provide the intravenous administration of drugs to patients who cannot take oral medication. Third, studies indicate that patients in the United States are reluctant to ask family or friends to assist them in suicide or to kill them. Consequently, they are likely to ask physicians to help them to do so. For such reasons, those who present this argument believe that it is critically important to have physicians involved in providing assisted suicide and euthanasia. Proponents of this position state that physicians should be allowed end patients' lives at their voluntary request or to put the means for doing this into their patients' hands.

4. The social context
a. The dangers of assisted suicide/euthanasia to the community can be overcome

Some who favor assisted suicide/euthanasia recognize that there is a legitimate concern that adopting these practices as a matter of policy and law would present dangers to society. Patients might have their lives ended without their request or under different circumstances than those they had requested when competent. They might be induced to end their lives by force or duress. Further, some who accept assisted suicide/euthanasia acknowledge that it is a realistic fear that the institutionalization of these practices would undercut the value of human life and could create patterns of practice that reflect a calculus of worth based on social usefulness.

However, the failure to legitimate assisted suicide/euthanasia, these proponents of assisted suicide/euthanasia point out, also has its dangers. Such failure could lead to secret and uncontrolled killing according to no agreed criteria. They also note that the "slippery slope" argument so frequently invoked by those opposed to assisted suicide/euthanasia—that allowing these acts could lead to involuntary or nonvoluntary euthanasia—is highly speculative. There are no data indicating how likely and widespread abuses and unwarranted extensions of these practices would be.

To avoid serious abuses of assisted suicide/euthanasia and the devaluation of human life, supporters of these acts state, these practices would have to be carefully regulated by law.[55] The Dutch have established conditions that physicians must meet before they provide euthanasia or else risk legal prosecution. While there have been cases where patients have been killed without a contemporaneous request in Holland,[56] in many of these instances patients had made such a request earlier and were not able to repeat it at the time of death. Strong and effective safeguards that provide independent monitoring of physician-assisted death can reasonably meet concerns about a slippery slope, advocates of assisted suicide/euthanasia believe.

b. Precautions can be taken against financial coercion of the critically ill into assisted suicide/euthanasia

Another legitimate concern acknowledged by proponents of assisted suicide/euthanasia is that those who are seriously ill might be pressured to end their lives by financially burdened relatives. Moreover, a health care system that is attempting to lower costs might subtly coerce those who are dying into doing so more quickly. Christians are called to protect the sick from forceful influences that would have them end their lives inappropriately. Consequently, some who accept assisted suicide/euthanasia hold that it is essential to enact regulations to provide safeguards against financially coerced decisions to end their lives by those who are near death. These regulations should provide stringent protections for those who choose to bring about their deaths directly, rather than die in great pain and suffering.

Even so, these proponents of assisted suicide/euthanasia state, it can be appropriate for individuals voluntarily to take financial considerations into account. The Ninth Circuit Federal Court of Appeals, for instance, acknowledged that some terminally ill adults might request a lethal dose of medication in order to protect their families from the expense of prolonged treatment. The court indicated that this would not be unrealistic. It was "reluctant to say that, in a society in which the costs of protracted health care can be so exorbitant, it is improper for competent, terminally ill adults to take the economic welfare of their families and loved ones into consideration."[57] Consideration of the needs of others is an appropriate Christian motive for electing assisted suicide or euthanasia, some therefore conclude.

5. Concluding statement on accepting assisted suicide/euthanasia

The primary reasons given by Christians for accepting assisted suicide and euthanasia focus on individual self-determination, human dignity, and compassion. Those who support these practices believe that we are in a fundamentally new situation today that requires us to rethink the implications of our traditional Christian ethic. We can now extend the time between the beginning and end of a serious, and ultimately terminal, illness to many months or even years. This power is not to be attributed to nature or the will of God, but to an almost Promethean effort on the part of human beings to avoid death. This new phase that we have added onto life, however, can become an intolerable burden for some people.

In the face of this new situation, the ultimate criterion for Christians must not be the maximal prolongation of biological life, but the realization of those values to which biological life is subordinate. Not every suicide or act of euthanasia is to be rejected as immoral, they argue. Instead, each must be judged on the basis of an evaluation of the benefits and burdens to the person involved in remaining alive. Those patients who meet certain conditions, such as being terminally or incurably ill, ought to be allowed to choose an elective death, proponents of assisted suicide/euthanasia hold. A Christian ethic that attempts to be both scriptural and contemporary, they maintain, will support a responsible decision to end human life by means of assisted suicide/euthanasia.[58] ■

Arguments for Rejecting Assisted Suicide/Euthanasia

The same features of contemporary life that have given force to the drive to accept assisted suicide/euthanasia are taken into account by Christians who believe these acts are wrong. Opponents of assisted suicide/euthanasia, however, do not find that these features justify discarding the long-standing Christian position against suicide and euthanasia. Their most significant arguments focus on 1) God's purposes for us and for the world and 2) the meaning and role of suffering in human life. The Christian view of autonomy, concern about pressure on the critically ill to justify remaining alive, and the dangers of abuse of the elderly, vulnerable, and disabled give added force to their position.

1. God's purposes
a. God's purposes would be impeded and God's sovereignty violated if assisted suicide/euthanasia were condoned

Our lives belong to God. As St. Paul declares, "Or do you not know that your body is a temple of the Holy Spirit within you, which you have from God, and that you are not your own? For you were bought with a price; therefore glorify God in your body" (1 Corinthians 6:19-20). We hold our lives in trust and are accountable to God for how we live them—and for how we die.

God's creative and loving purposes for us are the ultimate source of the inviolability of our lives. We intrude on those purposes when we deliberately end our lives, opponents of assisted suicide/euthanasia maintain. Doing so brings to an abrupt end our temporal opportunity to respond to God's call. Thus, we deny God's sovereignty when we carry our drive to control death to the point where we deliberately end our lives. The authors of

On Dying Well observed of the Christian, "he can claim no inalienable right to death on the grounds that his life is his own, and that after due consideration has been given to the interests of other men and women, he may do with it exactly as he pleases."[59]

Moreover, we are created by God to live in community with one another, caring for one another and working to achieve the common good. Robert Sanderson, a seventeenth century Anglican thinker stated:

> God hath made us sociable creatures, contrived us into policies and societies and commonwealths; made us fellow members of one body and every one another's members. As, therefore, we are not born, so neither must we live, to and for ourselves alone; but our parents and friends, and acquaintances nay, every man of us hath a kind of right and interest in every other man of us, and our country and the commonwealth in us all.[60]

The bonds that God has established between us would necessarily be diminished by assisted suicide/euthanasia, those opposed to these practices maintain. Such acts would introduce socially-sanctioned killing of the innocent into society and would cut out of human fellowship those most in need of it. This is among the major reasons that the Christian tradition has held that it is wrong deliberately to end innocent human life. [See C. Views about Ending and Extending Life in the Christian Tradition.]

The *Newark Report* has argued that the doctrine of creation opens the door to assisted suicide, for "[i]t is inherent in nature that life can be sustained only at the expense of other life."[61] This suggests that we should accept that killing is built into the very nature of things. Living in this world, on this view, involves a struggle in which the weak are destroyed by the strong. However, such a Nietzschean approach, which later generated Social Darwinist views requiring the elimination of the "unfit," is contrary to the Christian view of the goodness of God's creation. Moreover, a doctrine of creation cannot in itself mark out what is right and what is wrong about assisted suicide/euthanasia.[62] Further principles for determining the morality of these acts are necessary, opponents of assisted suicide/euthanasia point out.

Some advocates of assisted suicide/euthanasia have coupled a doctrine of creation with utilitarian principles justifying an act if it would bring about good consequences. The *Newark Report* would condone the willful taking of life "only if the good desired outweighs the potential evil and only if that good cannot be achieved in a less destructive manner."[63] This sort of calculation, however, could justify killing patients when their hospital or nursing home care is too burdensome for their families or society, critics declare. It could unacceptably jeopardize the lives of many, including those who are suffering from full-blown Alzheimer's disease and those who are severely disabled physically and in need of daily assistance. The Christian tradition does not accept a consequentialist calculus of benefits and burdens as the basis for determining who should live and who should die, those who oppose assisted suicide/euthanasia state. Instead, it holds that intentionally killing the innocent and committing suicide are wrong in themselves, even if they lead to some good consequences.

b. Some pain and suffering is inevitable; we are called to alleviate it through morally acceptable means, rather than by killing

Anyone who has accompanied a dying relative or friend knows the pain and suffering a death can bring. Faith in God's goodness and love does not wholly eliminate the sense of affliction, desolation, and isolation that some experience at the time of death. The threat of losing the relationships that give meaning and value to our lives creates immense suffering both for the dying and for those who keep watch. Grief, loss, and mental and spiritual anguish are unavoidable for those involved. Because we are finite and limited beings, such suffering is an inevitable consequence of our human condition. Throughout the history of the church, Christians have struggled to understand its meaning and its mystery.

The question in the scriptures is not whether we should suffer, but how and why. What is worth suffering for, and how might believers make sense of it?[64] Suffering can sanctify and transform us, those who reject assisted suicide/euthanasia declare. It can give us a clearer perspective on the meaning of our lives and on eternal life, show us our limitations, refine our faith, make us more Christlike, and produce perseverance and character (2 Corinthians 12:7-10; 1 Peter 1:5-7; Hebrews 12:1; Romans 5:3-5; Psalm 119:71). Coping with suffering constructively provides a better way to appreciate the love and presence of God than suicide, those opposed to assisted suicide/euthanasia argue, for even as we suffer, and ultimately as we die, God seeks to draw us to God and each other. God in Christ shares in our brokenness and suffering and calls us to share in God's.[65]

Much suffering is redemptive,[66] those who oppose assisted suicide/euthanasia hold, not just that which is explicitly borne for the sake of Christ. Paul did not indicate that Christians are to endure suffering *only when* it is for the Gospel, they note. He also emphasized the need to accept suffering that is caused by what appears, in his case, to have been a physical illness or condition. When he asked God to remove "a thorn" given him "in the flesh," he reported, "Three times I appealed to the Lord about this, that it would leave me, but he said to me, My grace is sufficient for you, for power is made perfect in weakness'" (2 Corinthians 12:7-9). A long tradition of Christian piety follows from Paul's example of coping with illness and suffering.

It is immensely important to recognize, however, that we are not obligated to endure all suffering that befalls us, those who oppose assisted suicide/euthanasia maintain. We have been brought into this world to prevent or end suffering where we can do so through moral means. Much of the pain and suffering that some who are seriously ill undergo today is due to inadequate pain relief and poor palliative care. Such suffering should be alleviated by medical and pastoral means—not by killing those who experience it, opponents of assisted suicide/euthanasia argue. [See F. 3. a. Correcting current undertreatment of pain and suffering would decrease requests for assisted suicide/euthanasia and F. 4. c. The social isolation of the elderly and dying makes them especially vulnerable to assisted suicide/euthanasia.]

Suffering is also due to the frequent failure of the Christian community to keep company with the dying.[67] We are called as a community in the Christian tradition to embody relations of trust, care, and mutual dependence. Where suffering is unavoidable and cannot rightly be averted or eliminated, it is to be shared in compassionate stewardship. Compassion for the sick and dying is essential to Christ's message in the Beatitudes and in the parable of the Good Samaritan. Compassion, however, does not automatically render any action that it motivates morally right, those who reject assisted suicide/euthanasia observe. It does not, for instance, justify shooting a wife-beater out of compassion for his victim. In itself, compassion for those who are in pain and suffering cannot justify assisted suicide or euthanasia, opponents of these practices maintain.

2. Human choice
a. Christian moral constraints on autonomy work against allowing assisted suicide/euthanasia

To acknowledge the importance of human freedom of choice is to recognize the great worth and dignity that God has bestowed on us. Yet the sheer fact that a choice for death is ours does not make it right. The God whom we love is the God "whose service is perfect freedom." This freedom, however, is not the freedom to do whatever we wish. When Jesus declared near the point of his death, "Father, into your hands I commend my spirit" (Luke 23:46), his free choice was willingly guided by God's purposes. Christian values and virtues should similarly inform and govern our choices about the end of life, those who reject assisted suicide/euthanasia argue. Our call to live out God's purposes in the world places moral constraints on what we may choose. Opponents of assisted suicide/euthanasia hold that the Christian prohibition of these practices is one such moral constraint.

Moreover, they argue, the "dominion" that God gave us in Genesis 1:28 does not mean that we are to take complete control of our own living—and of our dying. Instead, that "dominion" is better understood as taking responsibility for stewardship in this world, as we live in community with one another. We are to cede some of our autonomy, according to God's plan, for the good of the community. And that good would be seriously injured were we to allow socially-sanctioned killing of the innocent through assisted suicide/euthanasia, opponents of these practices believe. [See F.1.a. God's purposes would be impeded and God's sovereignty violated if assisted suicide/euthanasia were condoned.]

The *Newark Report* recognizes that we cannot choose to act in whatever way we desire. That report limits its approval of assisted suicide to those who are terminally ill or incurable.[68] But these particular boundaries on human freedom of choice are not rooted in any larger moral and theological framework in that report. What reasons have we for not allowing those who are curable to kill themselves if they do not wish to go through the period of pain and suffering that their treatment would involve? Without an understanding of the limited nature of human autonomy and dominion there is no reason to say "No" to such morally objectionable proposals, opponents of assisted suicide/euthanasia declare.

b. The availability of assisted suicide/euthanasia would eliminate our choice to remain alive without having to justify our existence

While the availability of assisted suicide/euthanasia might increase the choices open to us in certain respects, it would decrease our choices in others, some who reject these practices maintain. It would eliminate our choice to remain alive without having to justify our very existence. Given the option of assisted suicide/euthanasia, we could choose not to be killed—but to make that choice would render us accountable for choosing to live. Social expectations can well become a form of coercion, opponents of assisted suicide/euthanasia observe. Having the choice of assisted suicide/euthanasia would create pressure on us to decide to end our lives or else explain why we should remain alive.[69] How can we respond to the implicit question, "Why aren't you dead yet?"

Knowing that assisted suicide/euthanasia were available to us would make it more difficult for us to refuse the choice of death. It would eliminate our option of receiving life as a given. Rather than pressure patients to defend their decisions to remain alive, we ought to pressure our society to provide better support of seriously ill patients, critics of assisted suicide/euthanasia hold.

3. The impact of contemporary medicine

a. Appropriate treatment of pain and suffering would decrease requests for assisted suicide/euthanasia

Contrary to popular belief, patients in severe pain are *less* likely to approve of assisted suicide or euthanasia than patients who are not, according to a recent study of patients with cancer.[70] Patients are interested in getting rid of their pain—not in ending their lives. Yet despite tremendous technological advances in the treatment and prevention of pain, physicians' efforts to relieve physical pain and psychological suffering are, by and large, sadly deficient. Some physicians incorrectly fear that adequate use of opioids might induce addiction in dying patients and are concerned that providing adequate pain relief that depresses respiration might be viewed as a form of euthanasia.

Experts in pain management and palliative care maintain that currently available measures, if used appropriately, could relieve the pain and suffering of almost all dying persons, no matter how severe. One pain expert reports:

> We frequently see patients referred to our Pain Clinic who have considered suicide as an option, or who require physician-assisted suicide because of uncontrolled pain. We commonly see such ideation and request dissolve with adequate control of pain and other symptoms, using combinations of pharmacologic, neurosurgical, anesthetic or psychological approaches.[71]

The dying can be made comfortable while remaining conscious *if* adequate pain relief and palliative care are provided.[72] Should it become necessary to alleviate pain by using drugs that render patients unconscious or that might depress their respiration in the process, using such drugs remains morally acceptable and appropriate. [See B. 2. above, The distinction between providing adequate pain relief to the dying and assisted suicide/euthanasia.]

The fear of pain and suffering of those who are dying can be diminished by caregivers who develop an individualized plan for pain relief and comfort care with them. An inter-disciplinary palliative care team working with these patients, their families, other health care professionals, and pastoral counselors can provide them with continuing supportive care. In the long run, the anxiety of the dying about pain can be overcome by ensuring that physicians and nurses receive adequate training in pain management and by working to increase awareness, availability, and use of hospice programs.

We have the ability to relieve much of the pain and suffering of those who are dying and assist them to have a good death without taking their lives, many who reject assisted suicide/euthanasia argue. Brody, a physician and medical ethicist, states that "The ideal state of medical practice would be when active euthanasia is shunned by all physicians because to perform it would be to admit gross clinical incompetence, there existing so many better treatments for dying patients of all types and under all circumstances."[73] To this, others would add that we also need a system of care that provides better social support to seriously ill patients and their families.

b. The role of the physician is to heal, not to kill

Taking human life is antithetical to the work of healing and relieving suffering that is essential to the role of the physician, opponents of assisted suicide/euthanasia maintain. They maintain that the *Newark Report* is mistaken when it claims that assisted suicide is "part of the healing process because it enables the person to die well."[74] To combine killing with healing would result in confusion and distrust of doctors among patients; it would radically undermine the doctor-patient relationship. They argue that health care professionals should not become the agents of death.

Physicians have always been reluctant to participate in euthanasia, opponents of this practice state. When the emperor Hadrian, for example, asked his physician for assistance in committing suicide, the physician would not comply. When Napoleon asked his physician to provide deadly drugs to several extremely ill soldiers, the doctor refused. He declared that his obligation was to treat people, not kill them. The shadow of the Holocaust in Nazi Germany hangs over the discussion of assisted suicide/euthanasia. In that period, doctors began the killings with those who were incurably ill and then went on to kill Jews,

Gypsies, religious dissenters, and others who were "unfit to live."[75] The internalized barriers against harm to patients that are a crucial virtue of the medical profession were subverted in many doctors. As a result, they betrayed the trust of those who turned to them for care.

Physicians have been among the leaders in declaring that doctors must not terminate the lives of their patients.[76] Accepting physician-assisted suicide and euthanasia, opponents of these practices argue, would require a sweeping transformation of the very meaning of medicine and of the doctor-patient relationship. They aver that physicians have a professional calling to cure when possible, to care always, but never to kill.

c. Other means can be used to respond to the overuse of medical technology than assisted suicide/euthanasia

We have made major strides in fending off death through the use of modern medical technology and other medical practices. Yet this very technology can mask the inevitability of death and rob us of a good death. As the *Newark Report* observes, "[m]odern technology has created a dissonance with the past" and "[c]ontemporary medicine has generated a variety of choices previously unavailable to the individual."[77] These features of the current medical context, however, do not in themselves justify assisted suicide or euthanasia, opponents of these practices argue.

Ironically, assisted suicide/euthanasia represent yet another "technological fix" for the current dilemmas of the seriously ill and dying, opponents maintain. We have tended blindly to adopt a broad view that medical technology alone gives life and death. Acceptance of assisted suicide/euthanasia would amount to a capitulation to this skewed view and would render us objects to be employed in the service of an unrelenting medical machinery. Yet our experience of illness and aging should remind us that even with the variety of medical choices available, we are not in complete control of our lives—or of our deaths. Any power we assert over our dying is limited and qualified, critics of assisted suicide/euthanasia find. Our dependence is a challenge to hold fast to a power beyond our control who cherishes and values us. The rejection of our dependency through the overuse of medical technology and other medical treatments, they hold, amounts to rejection of our creaturehood and our interdependence.

Assisted suicide and euthanasia do not offer an adequate or moral response to the overuse of medical technology, those who reject these acts claim. A narrow focus on these practices blunts a broader focus on the issue of what is needed in order to honor the person and provide care in death and dying. Rather than ask whether to kill those who are dying, the question to pose is how a person should be cared for as death draws near. We can honor advance directives in which patients have indicated that they wish to avoid a prolonged period of technologically-assisted dying.[78] We can encourage them to talk with professional caregivers and family about the degree of technological support they want at the end of life. Further, we can offer those near death with hospice care, which provides physical, emotional, and spiritual support when life-sustaining technology is deemed morally inappropriate.[79] A major problem that introducing assisted suicide/euthanasia would create is that it would decrease society's motivation to provide these morally preferable alternatives to killing, critics of assisted suicide/euthanasia state.

4. The social context
a. Assisted suicide/euthanasia present individuals and society with dangers of abuse

It would be difficult—indeed, impossible, some maintain—to draw stable moral boundaries around assisted suicide/euthanasia were these practices sanctioned as a matter of public policy. After all, opponents ask, if a right to be killed is grounded in self-determination, why wait until individuals are dying before they can exercise that right? Why can they not choose to be killed earlier?[80] Although many proposals restrict these acts to the terminally ill, there is nothing inherent in the rationale of these proposals to prohibit the expansion of assisted suicide/euthanasia beyond terminal illness. Opponents argue that without any limiting principles, such an extension to the chronically ill and incurable seems inevitable.[81] [See above, F. 1. a. Christian moral constraints work against allowing assisted suicide/ euthanasia.]

Similar problems of delineating the criteria for eligibility for assisted suicide/euthanasia emerge in relation to a standard that requires some degree of pain and suffering before they could be provided, it is argued. These subjective experiences are difficult to assess and quantify. The Dutch, for instance, in at least one case, decided to view suffering as "unbearable" even when a patient had no physical disorder, but experienced psychosocial suffering relat-ed to a psychiatric disorder.[82] How are we to define that degree of physical or mental suffering that would justify killing the sufferer, those who reject assisted suicide/euthanasia ask.

Moreover, if the warrant for assisted suicide/euthanasia is to relieve suffering, there is no reason why these practices should be limited to those who are competent. Why not provide killing for those who are suffering and can no longer speak for themselves? If suffering provides a moral warrant for voluntary euthanasia, it should also provide a warrant for nonvoluntary euthanasia. This is acknowledged by Brock, a leading proponent of voluntary euthanasia, who states, "There is reason to expect that legaliza-tion of voluntary active euthanasia might soon be followed by strong pressure to legalize some nonvoluntary euthanasia of incompetent patients unable to express their own wishes."[83] One of the most serious problems with the thrust toward voluntary assisted suicide/euthanasia, those who reject them claim, lies in the jeopardy in which this places incompetent patients.

The experience of the Netherlands shows that nonvoluntary euthanasia can follow voluntary euthanasia, even when this is not planned. Although the Dutch guidelines require voluntary consent, there is clear evidence that incompetent patients and competent patients who have not requested it have received euthanasia.[84] Indeed, approximately two-thirds of nursing home residents in Holland indicate that they are afraid that their doc-tors may one day kill them.[85] The Dutch experience suggests that it is extremely difficult to restrict assisted suicide/euthanasia only to those who are dying. [See Appendix 2. Assisted Suicide/Euthanasia in the Netherlands.]

Once we cross the vital line between allowing to die and killing, where do we stop? Where does the slippery slope hit bottom?[86] To ask such questions is to expose the fragility of the limits suggested in proposals for assisted suicide/euthanasia, state those who reject these practices. Christians have a special responsibility to recognize our interrelatedness in Christ. Acts of assisted suicide and euthanasia threaten to destroy that interrelatedness and the very community at the heart of our faith by deliberately eliminating members essential to it.

b. Some persons would be pressured to end their lives for financial reasons if assisted suicide/euthanasia were available

As we move rapidly into managed care health plans, in which all the pressures are to cut costs, some who are critically ill may conclude that they cannot afford to remain alive. Assisted suicide/euthanasia may seem their only alternative. This may be the case for those lacking health care insurance for whom medical treatment, including palliative care, may not be available. Those among them who are terminally ill and have persistent and progressive pain may "voluntarily" choose assisted suicide or euthanasia because of financial pressures. Given the harsh economic realities that they must confront, however, it will be difficult to avoid the conclusion that they have been coerced and would not voluntarily embrace these acts.

Even those who have health care insurance may not feel assured that they will receive appropriate therapeutic and palliative care at the end of life. Hospital and physician financial incentives are changing. Under cost containment and managed care measures, the fewer the patients admitted to hospitals or referred to specialists, the greater the savings to health care systems and insurers. Moreover, physicians in some systems have an incentive to provide as little treatment as possible. In such environments, doctors who provide extensive treatment for their patients may jeopardize their hospital admitting privileges and managed care contracts because they impose high costs on their organization. Some therefore feel pressured to provide less treatment than they would otherwise.

In this climate of cost-cutting and profit-taking, assisted suicide/euthanasia can be seen as cheaper alternatives for health care systems than palliative care for the dying or ameliorative treatment for the incurable. Even if health care systems were prohibited by law from requiring assisted suicide/euthanasia for terminally ill or incurable patients, there would still be pressure on those near death to end their lives so that they do not become a financial liability to their families.[87] Questions of justice and fairness also are at issue. In a social context where medical care is already limited according to race, gender, and ability to pay, a policy of euthanasia might be implemented more readily for the poor, racial minorities, and women than for others.

To make assisted suicide/euthanasia available to those who are dependent, seriously ill, and without means to pay for additional care would place a morally unacceptable psychological and spiritual burden on them. Those who reject assisted suicide/euthanasia hold that we should not condone a practice that would push individuals to choose to die because they cannot afford to live.

c. **The social isolation of the dying, as well as the elderly and some with disabilities, may lead them inappropriately to choose assisted suicide/euthanasia**

The institutionalization of dying in our culture can create a profoundly alienating experience for many who are terminally ill. The elderly and persons with disabilities who are physically dependent can face lack of intergenerational companions and structural impediments in nursing homes and hospitals. Moreover, reports of abuse in nursing homes are on the increase.[88] The requests of persons in such institutions for assistance in killing themselves may arise, not from a fervent desire to leave this world, but from an experience of isolation, mistreatment, and dehumanization. We are created by God in a social dimension; our lives are built on mutual dependency. Therefore, we must ask whether the relational bonds of those requesting assisted suicide/euthanasia have been disrupted and whether such requests arise out of despair.

Assisted suicide/euthanasia would provide the final acts of isolation from others and from God for those who can no longer live self-contained lives, opponents of these practices argue. These acts would offer them a quick exit from a world in which human contact, affection, comfort, and care are lacking. "It would seem," the authors of *On Dying Well* observe, "that where there are other means available of exercising care and compassion toward a person in his dying and of relieving his ultimate distress, respect for God's creation and for the value of human life would tell against the practice of euthanasia or direct killing."[89]

Other means for exercising care and compassion are available, opponents of assisted suicide/euthanasia declare. The suffering of the dying, the elderly, and the disabled, rather than severing social relations, should provide an occasion for ministry that offers compassionate bonding, care, and fidelity. We can offer those who are terminally ill a presence that helps them affirm that none of us lives or dies to himself alone (Romans 14:7). We can provide an experience of God's care for them in the face of fear and sorrow as we share our faith and reassure those who are dying. Moreover, those who are at the end of life can offer gifts of love and faith to those of us in the Christian community who are open to receiving them.

5. Concluding statement on rejecting assisted suicide/euthanasia

People have always had to face the problem of pain and suffering at the end of life. From ancient Greece and Rome until today assisted suicide and euthanasia have been considered as ways of ending an extended period of dying. This is not a new issue raised within the last 50 years by our novel medical technology. "Indeed, almost all of the arguments made today to justify euthanasia were made before modern technology existed and could prolong life."[90] Surely, new circumstances and new knowledge give special force to the desire to ease the process of dying by ending life directly. However, these new factors provide no new circumstances or reasons for making a serious departure from the traditional Christian moral position that assisted suicide and euthanasia are contrary to God's loving purposes, those opposed to assisted suicide/euthanasia argue.

Should a moral quandary that arises in the most extreme situations at the end of life become the basis for a policy of killing? Christians are called to protect the weak and vulnerable from violations of their physical integrity, voluntary choice, and place within the community. The dangers of a policy that would promote assisted suicide/euthanasia for those at the edge of life, as well as the impossibility of regulating these practices, lead Christian and other critics to maintain that there are less drastic means of securing good care for those who are terminally ill than killing. We must recognize more openly that there comes a time when life is not being preserved, but death is being unnecessarily prevented and life should be allowed to come to its end. Those who are terminally ill deserve the full application of the vast array of measures for symptom control and palliative care that are currently available, as well as family and pastoral presence. We owe it to the dying to support and care for them as they pass through the valley of the shadow of death, not to kill them. ■

Arguments for Justifying or Excusing Assisted Suicide/Euthanasia in Rare, Extreme Circumstances

Some Christian thinkers who accept assisted suicide/euthanasia and some who reject these practices come remarkably close in their views. They meet in those extraordinary circumstances when the suffering of a dying patient has become intolerable and no means are available to alleviate it.

Some who accept assisted suicide/ euthanasia maintain that the Christian tradition should allow an exception to the prohibition against killing the innocent only in certain rare, extreme circumstances. Some who reject assisted suicide/euthanasia also hold that there are rare, extreme situations in which these acts should be allowed. While assisted suicide/euthanasia would violate the Christian prohibition against killing, they hold, this would be excusable. That is, they believe we would not be blameworthy for providing assisted suicide/euthanasia in such circumstances.

While both sets of thinkers hold that assisted suicide/ euthanasia should be provided in highly unusual circumstances, they differ in their explanation of why this would be morally acceptable. The first set holds that these acts would amount to a justified exception to the Christian prohibition of killing the innocent. The second set holds that these acts would be wrong, but would be excusable.

Both sets of thinkers hold that in some situations our pain and suffering may become so intense that it would be morally allowable for others to kill us or assist us in committing suicide. They ask, for example, Would it be wrong to ask a friend to kill us if we were trapped in a fiery car wreck with no way to escape? A loving, compassionate God "whose mercy endureth forever" would not will such an excruciatingly painful death for us, they believe. The same would seem true, they maintain, of certain extreme circumstances where those who are dying in pain and suffering contemplate suicide or euthanasia. The authors of *On Dying Well* suggest that there may be extraordinary cases in which the taking of human life is allowable when it prevents intolerable and uncontrollable suffering near death.[91]

Those who would allow assisted suicide/euthanasia in such extraordinary circumstances would recommend that the Episcopal Church acknowledge that there are circumstances in which 1) pain and suffering is extreme and unrelievable, 2) the patient is in the terminal stages of illness, and 3) suicide or killing are the only way to save the patient from an intolerable death. This would not apply to those who are dying slowly from a long-term illness, those who are in a persistent vegetative state, or those who are terminally ill and in pain, but not in unrelievable pain and suffering.

It is very important, however, to recognize that those who come to this conclusion mean it to apply only to the rare, extreme, and catastrophic case. Most instances of terminal illness are not analogous to the highly unusual case of burning to death, either in terms of the degree of pain and suffering involved or the nearness of death. Those allowing this justification or exception in extreme situations do not believe it would be morally acceptable to commit suicide when patients experience pain and suffering as part of the normal course of dying. They would instead call instead for better means of preventing such pain and suffering. Indeed, they might well agree with the spirit of the remark of Dean Inge, who seemed to accept assisted suicide/euthanasia in at least some instances, that "At the same time I hope, inconsistently perhaps, that if I were attacked by a painful illness I should have patience to wait for the end, and I do not think I should wish anyone near and dear to me to act otherwise."[92]

The authors of *On Dying Well* are concerned that justifying the compassionate killing of those who are dying in pain might lead to killing those who are not in extreme circumstances. They note, "...if the prohibition [against suicide and euthanasia] is qualified to allow for exceptional cases outside of those we normally encounter, it will be regarded as no longer binding in the ordinary conduct of life."[93] Wennberg, a Protestant minister, explains further that

[i]t is important to remind ourselves that there is a danger in doing ethics by relying heavily on extreme cases, and the case of the soldier who commits suicide as the only alternative to being burned alive in a tank is just such a case. By focusing on extreme cases, we can unfairly undermine confidence in the firmness of moral rules that in the context of normal human existence are in fact sound and virtually exceptionless.[94]

The Committee on Health, Human Values, and Ethics of the Episcopal Diocese of Southern Ohio provides a related approach in these rare, extreme circumstances. It states in a study document:

We believe that if medically assisted death is ever morally permissible, cases in which it is permissible are the exception and not the rule. And since exceptions must always be made on a case by case basis, after careful consideration of the circumstances of each individual case, we recommend that neither the church nor the state support decisions for medically assisted death by law or by policy. We also recommend that neither the church nor the state exceptionlessly prohibit such decisions.[95]

On this view, there is a presumption against the practice of assisted suicide/euthanasia, rather than a prohibition of them. That is, medically assisted death should not be chosen for the most part, but may be in some unusual circumstances. Assisted suicide/euthanasia are generally morally inappropriate forms of death for many of the reasons stated above in section F., on this approach, but they may be morally acceptable choices in some cases. A decision about when this is the case must be made in specific instances according to the practical wisdom of those with knowledge and experience in the sort of situation in question. As P.R. Baelz observed,

...there are others who believe that a deepening of moral insight demands that we discriminate between different cases, proscribe some and permit others, while recognizing that the complexity of the issues lays a heavy burden of decision on one or more individuals in any particular case.[96]

Yet decisions that seem morally acceptable in individual circumstances can slide into loose general policy that could lead to killing in cases where it would be clearly wrong. Therefore, this proposal would not recommend that the church accept assisted suicide/euthanasia as moral as a general rule. Nor would it recommend that the church prohibit these acts in all cases.

Others who view assisted suicide and euthanasia as wrong in all cases respond that justified or exceptional circumstances cannot be specified precisely enough. The class of rare cases is bound to expand continuously until its boundaries vanish, they fear. Moreover, they argue, in cases of extreme pain we can give currently available measures to relieve intolerable suffering, short of intending to kill the sufferer. Consequently, they would not recommend that the church recognize such rare circumstances as exceptions to the prohibition against assisted suicide/euthanasia or as excusable. ∎

H

Finding a Christian Approach to the Question of Assisted Suicide/Euthanasia

Paradoxically, those Christians who accept and those who reject assisted suicide and euthanasia begin with similar convictions. Both have a sense of the sovereignty of God. Both want to protect human dignity and to preserve the freedom of individual persons to choose how to confront human finitude and death. They both view life as a gift that is good, but not entirely at the disposal of humanity. Life is not another god, but a good in relationship to the broader purposes of life. These purposes, they agree, include bodily integrity, the integrity of the spirit, sharing in human community, and honoring and nurturing goods beyond the self. They recognize that human life, especially in situations of death and dying, often confronts us with a conflict of goods in which physical life clashes with other purposes or goods of life. Moreover, they are aware that advances in medical technology may be used to preserve and extend life apart from other goods of human life. They agree that the goals of medicine include the relief of suffering and the restoration of health, not simply the extension of physical life.

Both approaches also share certain Christian impulses and sensitivities. They feel compassion toward those who suffer near death and desire to relieve their suffering in ways consonant with God's purposes. Both call on health caregivers and pastoral counselors to improve their treatment of pain and suffering, not only pharmacologically, but psychologically and spiritually. And both recognize that Christian principles of social justice call us to attempt to remedy a public policy that provides inadequate social support not only to the large number of persons who are poor and very sick, but also to those who are better off financially, yet lack medical and social support during critical illness. They agree that Christ's charge to us to love our neighbor obligates us to look beyond our own health care needs to those of the community in which we are nourished.

However, there are central differences between them. One lies in the judgment they make about God's purposes and power in light of human suffering. Those who accept assisted suicide/euthanasia maintain that God's dominion over our lives does not require us to continue to live in pain and suffering. Instead, our duty of love toward one another calls us to assist those near death who are in agony to go on to eternal life quickly and directly. Those who are critical of assisted suicide/euthanasia maintain that our stewardship over life does not include the choice directly to end it. Killing is not the only alternative to allowing God's creatures to die a miserable death. Rather than kill, they believe, we must withdraw useless treatment and provide adequate pain relief and compassionate care and comfort to those who are dying.[97]

A second central difference lies in their evaluation of whether adequate safeguards can be built into a policy of assisted suicide/euthanasia. Christian proponents of these practices believe that strong and effective protections can be written into policies allowing them. Opponents, pointing to the experience of the Netherlands, maintain that such safeguards cannot be guaranteed and implemented and that once we start down the path that accepts killing, we will be impelled to extend it to the most vulnerable among us.

How are we within the Episcopal Church to resolve such differences and reach a final position? A recent Episcopal study group noted that:

> Differences in moral judgments are not simply or narrowly matters of right and wrong. Rather, differences in judgment reflect differences in understandings that can be articulated, respected, and debated… Christian ethics and moral theology provide the basis for critical reflection that informs moral judgments and promotes respect for those who may differ.[98]

When disagreement about a significant moral issue such as assisted suicide/euthanasia persists, even in light of central Christian teachings, we have a responsibility to explore avenues of common ground as we weigh arguments on all sides.

Further, we must recognize, no matter which side we take, that those with whom we disagree about this difficult matter are working in good conscience to keep faith with God. And those with whom we agree are to be encouraged, as Kenneth Kirk observed, to realize that moral truth can have some uncertainties attached to it due to "the limitations of the human mind, the imperfection of the human vocabulary, and the needs of different ages."[99] More recently, Sedgwick has stressed the dynamic, historical character of the gift of Christian faith, suggesting that "we have more and more come to understand ourselves not as applying rules to situations but as responding to actions in light of our interpretations and expectations which themselves are given by the community in which we share our lives."[100] Ultimately, however, as Bishop Kirk maintains:

> It is the main bulwark of the Christian position that duty is not something as to which a man has the right to choose or create the claims that he is going to recognize, but that it is something there—something outside ourselves—something the same for all—something in the eternal will of God—for us to discover and obey.[101]

We present this report with the hope and prayer that it will lead readers to take a closer look at the issue of assisted suicide/ euthanasia from a Christian perspective. We do not mean to end discussion and argument, but to encourage communication and debate. We suggest that as we reflect on this issue, we confer with family, pastors, physicians, friends, and others. Only through engaging in dialogue will we discover that "something outside ourselves—something the same for all—something in the eternal will of God" that points to the approach that we should take to assisted suicide and euthanasia. Such an approach will lead us to take account of the underlying, broader question concerning care for the critically ill and dying: How can we enable one another to die a good Christian death? ■

Notes

1.   *Report of the Task Force on Assisted Suicide to the 122nd Convention of the Episcopal Diocese of Newark*, January 27, 1996. [Hereafter referred to as *Newark Report*.]

2.   See Kenneth E. Kirk, *Some Principles of Moral Theology and their Application* (London: Longmans, 1920); Frederick Denison Maurice, *The Kingdom of Christ*, vol. II (London: SCM Press, 1958), p. 331; David H. Smith, *Health and Medicine in the Anglican Tradition* (New York: Crossroad, 1986); Timothy Sedgwick and Philip Turner, eds., *The Crisis in Moral Teaching in the Episcopal Church* (Harrisburg, PA: Morehouse, 1992).

3.   Stephen Sykes and John Booty, eds., *The Study of Anglicanism* (London and Philadelphia: SPCK and Fortress, 1988), Part III.

4.   Gordon R. Dunstan, *The Artifice of Ethics* (London: SCM Press, 1974), p. 52; "The Authority of a Moral Claim: Ian Ramsey and the Practice of Medicine," *Journal of Medical Ethics* 13 (1987): 189-94.

5.   David Brown, *Choices: Ethics and the Christian* (Oxford: Blackwell, 1983), pp. 25-53; David H. Smith, pp. 5-20.

6.   J.F.D. Maurice, *The Kingdom of Christ* (London: SPCK, 1958) vol. I, pp. 226-33.

7.   Richard Hooker, *Laws of Ecclesiastical Polity*, Sixth Edition (Oxford: Keble, 1874), v. 54.4. Quoted in David H. Smith, p. 9.

8.   Tom L. Beauchamp and James F. Childress, *Principles of Biomedical Ethics*, 4th Ed. (New York: Oxford, 1994), pp. 120-132; James F. Childress, "The Place of Autonomy in Bioethics," *Hastings Center Report* 20(1) (1990): 12-16.

9.   Daniel Callahan, *The Troubled Dream of Life* (New York: Simon and Schuster, 1993), pp. 42-48, 91-119.

10. New York State Task Force on Life and the Law, *When Death Is Sought: Assisted Suicide and Euthanasia in the Medical Context*, May, 1994 (New York State Task Force on Life and the Law, 5 Penn Plaza, New York, N.Y. 1001-1803), pp. 35-48.

11. President's Commission for the Study of Ethical Problems in Medicine and Biomedical ad Behavioral Research, *Deciding to Forego Life-Sustaining Treatment* (Washington, D.C.: U.S. Government Printing Office, 1983), pp. 100-18.

12. Daniel P. Sulmasy, "Managed Care and Managed Death," *Archives of Internal Medicine* 155(2) (1995): 133-36; P.A. Singer and M. Siegler, "Euthanasia—A Critique," *New England Journal of Medicine* 322 (1990): 1881-83; R.I. Misbin, "Physicians' Aid in Dying," *New England Journal of Medicine* 235 (1991): 1307-11.

13. James F. Gustafson, *Ethics from a Theocentric Perspective*, vol. II (University of Chicago Press, 1984), pp. 187-216.

14. The *Newark Report*, in referring to euthanasia as "any intervention which lessens the suffering of illness; an intervention that at times carries with it the danger of terminating life prematurely," (p. 2) conflates several different understandings of euthanasia. Euthanasia requires an intent to terminate life. The definition provided in the *Newark Report* could imply that providing even minor analgesia for someone who is ill is a form of euthanasia.

15. Tom L. Beauchamp, "Introduction," *Intending Death: The Ethics of Assisted Suicide and Euthanasia*, ed. Tom L. Beauchamp (Upper Saddle River, New Jersey: Prentice Hall, 1996), pp. 1-22.

16. *Newark Report*, p. 8.

17. Maurice A. M. de Wachter, "Euthanasia in The Netherlands," *Hastings Center Report* 22 (1992): 23-30.

18. See Robert D. Truog, Charles B. Berde, Christine Mitchell, Holcombe E. Grier, "Barbiturates in the Care of the Terminally Ill," *New England Journal of Medicine* 327(23) (1992): 1678-82.

19. Kenneth E. Kirk, *Conscience and Its Problems: An Introduction to Casuistry* (London: Longmans, Green, 1927), p. 8.

20. Michael Bratman, *Intentions, Plans and Practical Reason* (Cambridge, Mass.: Harvard University Press, 1987), pp. 16-17.

21. General Synod Board for Social Responsibility, *On Dying Well. An Anglican Contribution to the Debate on Euthanasia* (Newport and London: Church Information Office, 1975), p. 9. [Hereafter referred to as *On Dying Well.*]

22. Ibid., p. 61.

23. Dan Brock, "Voluntary Active Euthanasia," *Hastings Center Report* 22(2) (1992): 10-22.

24. Darrel W. Amundsen, "Suicide and Early Christian Values," in Baruch A. Brody, ed., *Suicide and Euthanasia* (Dordrecht, Netherlands: Kluwer, 1989), pp. 77-153.

25. Gary B. Ferngren, "Ethics of Suicide in Renaissance and Reformation," in Baruch A. Brody, ed., *Suicide and Euthanasia* (Dordrecht, Netherlands: Kluwer, 1989), pp. 155-181.

26. Hastings Rashdall, *The Theory of Good and Evil: A Treatise on Moral Philosophy* (Oxford: Clarendon Press, 1907), vol. 1, pp. 208-12.

27. W.R. Inge, *Christian Ethics and Moral Problems* (New York: Putnam, 1930).

28. Joseph Fletcher, *Morals and Medicine* (Princeton, New Jersey: Princeton University Press, 1954). Dr. Fletcher, an Episcopal priest and theologian with a special focus on medical ethics, left the Christian church in the latter part of his life.

29. Harold Y. Vanderpool, "Death and Dying: Euthanasia and Sustaining Life: I. Historical Aspects," *Encyclopedia of Bioethics*, revised edition, vol. 1, (New York: Macmillan, 1995), pp. 554-63.

30. Thomas Wood, "Homicide," *Westminster Dictionary of Christian Ethics*, James F. Childress and John Macquarrie, eds. (Philadelphia: Westminster Press, 1986), pp. 270-71.

31. Fletcher, *Morals and Medicine*, pp. 172-210.

32. Smith, p. 66.

33. Thomas Wood, "Euthanasia," *Westminster Dictionary of Christian Ethics*, James F. Childress and John Macquarrie, eds. (Philadelphia: Westminster Press, 1986), pp. 210-12.

34. James F. Childress, "Life, Prolongation of," *Westminster Dictionary of Christian Ethics*, James F. Childress and John Macquarrie, eds. (Philadelphia: Westminster Press, 1986), pp. 349-350.

35. Brock, p. 17.

36. Hans Küng, "A Dignified Dying," in Hans Küng and Walter Jens, *Dying with Dignity* (New York: Continuum, 1995), p. 26.

37. *Newark Report*, p. 8.

38. Ibid., 9.

39. Fletcher, *Morals and Medicine*, pp. 195-96.

40. *Newark Report*, p. 4.

41. *On Dying Well*, p. 18.

42. Hastings Rashdall, p. 208.

43. Wendy Farley, *Tragic Vision and Divine Compassion: A Contemporary Theodicy* (Westminster/John Knox Press: Louisville, Kentucky, 1990), p. 21.

44. W.R. Inge, p. 397.

45. *Newark Report*, p. 5.

46. Ibid., p. 7.

47. Joseph Fletcher, *Situation Ethics* (Philadelphia: Westminster Press, 1966), p. 30.

48. Fletcher, *Morals and Medicine*, pp. 183-84, 197.

49. John S. Spong, "In Defense of Assisted Suicide," Supplement to the *Newark Report*.

50. Fletcher, *Morals and Medicine*, p. 191.

51. Larry Falkowski, "A Conversation with the Rev. Larry Falkowski, Ph.D.", *The CHAPLAIR of the Assembly of Episcopal Hospitals and Chaplains*, Spring, 1996, p. D.

52. Note, "Physician-Assisted Suicide and the Right to Die with Assistance," *Harvard Law Review* 105 (1992):2021-2039.

53. Anthony L. Back, Jeffrey I. Wallace, Helene E. Starks, Robert A. Pearlman, "Physician-Assisted Suicide and Euthanasia in Washington State," *Journal of the American Medical Association* 275(12) (1996): 919-925; Diane E. Meier, "Doctors' Attitudes and Experiences with Physician-Assisted Death: A Review of the Literature." In J.M. Humber, R.F. Almeder, G.A. Kasting, eds., *Physician-Assisted Death* (Totowa, New Jersey: Humana Press, 1994), pp. 5-24.

54. Charles H. Baron, Clyde Bergstresser, Dan W. Brock, Garrick F. Cole, Nancy S. Dorfman, Judith A. Johnson, Lowell E. Schnipper, James Vorenberg, Sidney H. Wanzer, "A Model State Act to Authorize and Regulate Physician-Assisted Suicide," *Harvard Journal on Legislation* 33 (1996): 1-33.

55. Franklin G. Miller, Timothy E. Quill, Howard Brody, John G. Fletcher, Lawrence O. Gostin, Diane E. Meier, "Regulating Physician-Assisted Death," *New England Journal of Medicine* 331(2) (1994): 119-23.

56. Carlos F. Gomez, *Regulating Death* (New York: Free Press, 1991); Margaret Battin, "Voluntary Euthanasia and the Risks of Abuse: Can We Learn Anything from the Netherlands?" *Law, Medicine, and Health Care* 20 (1992): pp. 133-43; L. Pijenborg, P.J. van der Maas, J.J.M. van Delden, C.W.N. Looman, "Life-Terminating Acts without Explicit Request of Patient," *Lancet* 341 (1993): 1196-99.

57. *Compassion in Dying v. State of Washington*, 85 F.3d 1440; 1996 U.S. App. LEXIS 14170.

58. See Küng, "A Dignified Dying," p. 33.

59. *On Dying Well*, p. 16.

60. Robert Sanderson, Sermon IV, *Sermons ad Populum Works*, vol. III, pp. 101ff. Quoted in Thomas Wood, *English Casuistical Divinity During the Seventeenth Century* (London: SPCK, 1952), pp. 58f.

61. *Newark Report*, p. 4. The *Newark Report* further observes that while *bios*, "the notion of life itself," is to be cherished, it must be placed in "creative tension" with *zoe*, "the sweetness and significance of life..." That report goes on to suggest that sharing in zoe may be compatible with choosing assisted suicide.

Some members of our committee and some consultants challenge this argument on a number of grounds. The most fundamental is that a supposed semantic distinction between Greek words is not a basis for setting aside the long-held Christian view that suicide and euthanasia are contrary to God's commands. To make such an argument, the authors of the *Newark Report* would need to show that early Christians understood the alleged distinction as they do.

These persons further point out that, according to Bauer, Arndt, and Gingrich's *A Greek-English Lexicon, bios* and *zoe* can both refer to earthly, physical life. Liddell and Scott's *Lexicon* distinguishes *zoe*, "animal life," from *bios*, "mode of life" in the entry under *bios*; under *zoe*, the entry makes clear the wider sense of this word as "Life/existence" (vs. "death"), or = *bios* "way of life." Thus, *bios* and *zoe* can be used synonymously to refer to physical existence and a putative distinction between them cannot provide firm grounds for claiming that assisted suicide and euthanasia are compatible with sharing in *zoe*.

Moreover, our consultants note, the Fourth Gospel declares that we are to follow God's commands if we are to share in *zoe*. To kill oneself or to have another do so, consequently, would be to estrange oneself from *zoe* and wrongly destroy God's gift of *bios*.

62. A statement in the 1975 Anglican report, *On Dying Well*, p. 22 is taken out of context in the *Newark Report* to support the latter's position condoning assisted suicide. This statement suggests that it could be a "morally creative act" to kill a dying person who feels "himself a burden to others as well as to himself." This represents one of an array of moral positions explored, but not endorsed, in the Anglican report. Indeed, the Anglican report maintains that there are strong grounds for upholding the principle forbidding killing human beings.

63. *Newark Report*, p. 4.

64. Sondra Ely Wheeler, *Stewards of Life: Bioethics and Pastoral Care* (Nashville: Abingdon, 1996), p. 33.

65. David H. Smith, pp. 6-8; David H. Smith, "Suffering, Medicine, and Christian Theology," *On Moral Medicine:*

Theological Perspectives in Medical Ethics, ed. Stephen E. Lammers and Allen Verhey (Grand Rapids, Michigan: Eerdmans, 1987), pp. 255-61; Arthur C. McGill, *Suffering: A Test of Theological Method* (Philadelphia: Westminster, 1982), pp. 10-11.

66. C. S. Lewis, *The Problem of Pain* (New York: Macmillan, 1943), p. 168.

67. Paul Ramsey, *The Patient as Person: Explorations in Medical Ethics* (New Haven:YaleUniversity Press, 1970).

68. A limit on patient autonomy often found in proposals for assisted suicide/euthanasia is that those requesting assistance must experience "severe," "unbearable," or "intolerable" pain. This requirement is absent from the *Newark Report*, which allows assisted suicide for any degree of ineliminable suffering. Persons with conditions that do not necessarily involve severe pain, such as certain forms of arthritis, diabetes, or kidney disease, could choose assisted suicide without moral wrongdoing on this standard. Further, most who favor assisted suicide require that those requesting it be free from mental illness and depression. That limit is also missing from the *Newark Report*. This is especially troubling, for the problems of psychiatric illness among those requesting assisted suicide and euthanasia are well known. See, for instance, Y. Conwell and E.D. Caine, "Rational Suicide and the Right to Die: Reality and Myth," *New England Journal of Medicine* 325 (1991): 1100-02.

69. Allen Verhey, "Choosing Death: The Ethics of Assisted Suicide," *Christian Century*, July 17-24, 1996, pp. 716-719.

70. E.J. Emanuel, D.L. Fairclough, E.R. Daniels, B.R. Clarridge, "Euthanasia and Physician Assisted Suicide: Attitudes and Experiences of Oncology Patients, Oncologists, and the Public," *Lancet*, 9018 (1996): 1805-10.

71. Kathleen Foley, "The Relationship of Pain and Symptom Management to Patient Requests for Physician-Assisted Suicide," *Journal of Pain and Symptom Management* 6 (1991): 289-97.

72.   Robert D. Truog, Charles B. Berde, "Pain, Euthanasia, and Anesthesiologists," *Anesthesiology* 78 (1993): 353-60.

73.   Howard Brody, *The Healer's Power* (New Haven: Yale University Press, 1992), pp. 81-82.

74.   *Newark Report*, p. 9.

75.   Cynthia B. Cohen, "The Nazi Analogy in Bioethics," *Hastings Center Report* 18(4) (1988):32-33.

76.   W. Gaylin, L. Kass, E.D. Pellegrino, M. Siegler, "Doctors Must Not Kill," *Journal of the American Medical Association* 259 (1988): 2139-40.

77.   *Newark Report*, p. 7.

78.   See Committee on Medical Ethics of the Episcopal Diocese of Washington, *Before You Need Them: Advance Directives for Health Care, Living Wills and Durable Powers of Attorney* (Cincinnati: Forward Movement Publications, 1995).

79.   Robert J. Miller, "Hospice Care as an Alternative to Euthanasia," *Law, Medicine, and Health Care* 20(1-2) (1992), 127-32.

80.   Daniel Callahan, "When Self-Determination Runs Amok," *Hastings Center Report* 22(2) (1992), pp. 52-55.

81.   An expansion of the usual conditions for assisted suicide/euthanasia is found in the *Newark Report*. There assisted suicide is accepted not only for the dying, but for those whose condition is "incurable" and whose pain and/or suffering is persistent or progressive and unrelievable. See *Newark Report*, p. 8.

82.   Herbert Hendin, "Seduced by Death: Doctors, Patients, and the Dutch Cure," *Issues in Law and Medicine* 10(2) (1994): 123-68.

83.   Brock, p. 20.

84. Paul J. van der Maas, Johannes J.M. van Delden, Loes Pijenborg, Caspar W.N. Looman, "Euthanasia and Other Medical Decisions Concerning the End of Life," *Lancet* 338 (1991): 669-74.

85. Maurice A.M. de Wachter, "Euthanasia in The Netherlands," *Hastings Center Report* 22(2) (1992): 23-30.

86. Hessel Bouma III, Douglas Diekema, Edward Langerak, Theodore Rottman, Allen Verhey, *Christian Faith, Health, and Medical Practice* (Grand Rapids, MI: Eerdmans, 1989), p. 300.

87. R.J. Blendon, U.S. Szalay, R.A. Knox, "Should Physicians Aid their Patients in Dying?" *Journal of the American Medical Association* 267 (1992): 2658-62; George J. Annas, "Death by Prescription—The Oregon Initiative, *New England Journal of Medicine* 331(18) (1994): 1240-43.

88. Marylou Tousignant and Patricia Davis, "Nursing Homes in Area, Nationwide Plagued by Reports of Abuse," *Washington Post*, October 13, 1996, B1.

89. *On Dying Well*, p. 18.

90. Ezekiel Emanuel, "The History of Euthanasia Debates in the United States and Britain," *Annals of Internal Medicine* 121(10) (1994): 793-802.

91. *On Dying Well*, pp. 10-12.

92. Inge, p. 373.

93. *On Dying Well*, p. 11.

94. Robert N. Wennberg, *Terminal Choices: Euthanasia, Suicide, and the Right to Die* (William B. Eerdmans, Grand Rapids, Michigan, 1989), pp. 86-7.

95. Committee on Health, Human Values, and Ethics of the Episcopal Diocese of Southern Ohio, "Response to the Resolution Concerning Assisted Suicide Adopted by the 122nd Convention of the Episcopal Diocese of Newark," February 23, 1996.

96. P.R. Baelz, "Voluntary Euthanasia: Some Theological Reflections," *Theology* 75 (1972): 238-51.

97. Susan M. Wolf, Cynthia B. Cohen, Bruce Jennings, Paul Homer, Daniel Callahan, and The Hastings Center Study Group, *Guidelines on the Termination of Life-Sustaining Treatment and the Care of the Dying* (Bloomington, Indiana: Indiana University, 1987).

98. Timothy Sedgwick, "Introduction," *The Crisis in Moral Teaching in the Episcopal Church*, Timothy Sedgwick and Philip Turner, eds., (Harrisburg, PA: Morehouse, 1992), pp. 9-10.

99. Kirk, *Conscience and Its Problems*, p. 79.

100. Timothy F. Sedgwick, "Revising Anglican Moral Theology," in *The Anglican Moral Choice*, Paul Elmen, ed. (Harrisburg, PA: Morehouse, 1983), pp. 121-140.

101. Kirk, *Conscience and Its Problems*, p. 33.

Appendices

1. Two recent federal courts of appeals decisions

Over the last two decades, the right of competent patients to forgo medical treatment has become recognized and legally sanctioned in court decisions and by statute. As this right to refuse treatment has become established in the law, the question has arisen whether the control of patients over their dying should be extended to permit them directly to end their lives with or without the help of others.

This issue is not only a source of ethical and religious controversy, it is also a matter of legal controversy. In 1996, two decisions from two different circuits of the federal courts of appeals in the United States were handed down on this issue. These courts ruled that laws in two states prohibiting physicians from providing lethal drugs to competent terminally ill patients who requested violated the Constitution. Both decisions are under review by the Supreme Court of the United States at the time of this writing.

Each case involved a challenge to a state statute which made it a criminal offense to assist a person in ending his or her life, regardless of that person's condition. The parties made the same two constitutional arguments in each case: due process of law and equal protection of law. Although the courts reached the same substantive conclusion, each did so on different grounds.

a. *Compassion in Dying v. State of Washington,* 85 F.3d 1440; 1996 U.S. App. LEXIS 14170

The Ninth Circuit Federal Court of Appeals cast the issue in terms of whether a person has the constitutionally protected right to choose the time and manner of his or her death. It held that there is a liberty interest in determining the time and manner of one's own death that is protected by the due process clause of the Fourteenth Amendment. This interest must be weighed against the state's interest in preserving human life.

The case was brought by four physicians, three terminally ill patients, and the organization, Compassion in Dying. The patients involved had less than six months to live. One had cancer and was in hospice care. Another had AIDS, and a third chronic obstructive lung disease. They stated that their pain was not fully alleviated by medication and they had other sorts of serious discomfort. The three patients died during earlier stages of the court proceedings.

The court modelled its decision after some of the decisions upholding the right to abortion. In *Casey*, a Supreme Court abortion decision, the Court said that the issues "involved the most intimate and personal choices a person may make in a lifetime, choices central to personal dignity and autonomy." (*Casey*, 112 S. Ct. at 2807.) The choice to die, the Ninth Circuit stated, is also one of the most intimate and personal choices a person may make in a lifetime. It is a choice central to personal dignity and autonomy.

The court incorporated a range of acts under the rubric of "the right to die," including the right to refuse or stop medical treatment and the right to receive pain-relieving medication, even though this may hasten death. Since these are covered by "the right to die," the court declared, assisted suicide should also be covered by this right, for these are all ways of hastening death. The court could see no difference between stopping treatment and allowing patients to die, and allowing patients to kill themselves. Nor could it see a difference between giving patients drugs meant to relieve pain that also hasten death and giving them lethal drugs with which to kill themselves. These acts have the same inevitable result, according to the court.

The Ninth Circuit restricted its conclusions to those who are terminally ill, which usually means those who will die within six months. The court declared that "[a] competent terminally ill adult, having lived nearly the full measure of his life, has a strong liberty interest in choosing a dignified and humane death rather than being reduced at the end of his existence to a childlike state of helplessness, diapered, sedated, incontinent. How a person dies not only determines the nature of the final period of his existence, but in many cases, the enduring memories held by those who love him." [78] This decision does not cover those like Janet Adkins, the first patient whom Dr. Kevorkian helped die, who are in the early stages of Alzheimer's.

However, people cannot just commit suicide with the help of a physician in any way and at any time they choose, according to the Ninth Circuit. The state can regulate assisted suicide, even though it cannot ban it entirely.

The conclusions of this court will hold for eight western states unless they are overturned by the United States Supreme Court.

b. *Quill v. Vacco*, 80 F.3d 716; 1996 U.S. App. LEXIS 6215

In the second decision, handed down by the Second Circuit in New York, the parties made the same arguments that were offered in *Compassion in Dying*. However, contrary to the holding of the Ninth Circuit, the court rejected the argument that assisted suicide is a fundamental right protected by the Constitution. In the opinion of this court, assisted suicide is neither readily identifiable in the constitution's text nor implicit in the concept of ordered liberty. Therefore it does not qualify as a fundamental right protected by the due process clause of the Fourteenth Amendment.

The Second Circuit did embrace the Equal Protection argument, an argument on which the Ninth Circuit had declined to rule. It found that the New York statue criminalizing assisted suicide did not treat equally all competent persons who are terminally ill and want to hasten their deaths. It concluded that the distinction made in state law between similarly situated persons did not further any legitimate purpose. That is, the New York state law allowed terminally ill patients who were receiving life-sustaining treatment to have it removed so that they could hasten their deaths. However, it did not allow terminally ill patients who were *not* receiving such treatment to hasten their deaths in ways of their own choosing. Yet "[b]y ordering the discontinuance of these artificial life-sustaining processes or refusing to accept them in the first place, a patient hastens his death by means that are not natural in any sense." Therefore, the court concluded, the state law lacked any rational basis and it violated the Equal Protection Clause of the Constitution.

c. Final Comments

Although the Second and Ninth Circuits adopted different legal grounds for their conclusions, their construction of the basic issue was the same. For both courts, there is no difference between forgoing medical treatment and thereby insuring one's death, and using medical treatment to secure one's death. In both instances, the patient dies, not from the disease, but from how he or she uses medical technology. In both instances, the cause of death is the patient's decision to put an end to his or her own existence.

Both decisions apply only to doctors and not to others who might help a person commit suicide.

2. Assisted suicide/euthanasia in the Netherlands

Euthanasia by administering lethal drugs at the patient's request has been carried out openly by physicians in the Netherlands since the 1980s. Although euthanasia is illegal in Holland, and can result in up to twelve years' imprisonment, doctors will not be criminally prosecuted if they follow a policy established in 1985. This policy requires that physicians performing euthanasia have a long-standing clinical relationship with the patient, and that the patient must suffer pain that cannot be relieved and must repeatedly ask for death.

More specifically, Dutch guidelines require:

1. *Competence.* Euthanasia is to be performed only on a fully informed and competent adult.

2. *Voluntariness.* The patient's request must be voluntary, persistent, and conscious. It must be made repeatedly and must be documented.

3. *Unconditional suffering.* The patient must experience suffering that cannot be relieved by any other means. Both physician and patient must consider the patient's condition to be beyond recovery, although the patient need not be terminally ill.

4. *Consultation.* The attending physician must consult with another physician regarding the patient's condition and the genuineness and appropriateness of the request for euthanasia.

The Dutch do not require that the patient must be terminally ill. They allow a broad definition of suffering that includes mental suffering even when the patient has no physical disorder. [See Maurice A.M. de Wachter, "Euthanasia in The Netherlands," *Hastings Center Report* 22 (1992): 23-30.] The usual method of euthanasia is to induce sleep with barbiturates followed by a lethal injection of curare.

How often is euthanasia performed in Holland? A 1991 report, the Remmelink Report, which was sponsored by the government of the Netherlands, indicated that euthanasia accounted for about 2,300 deaths in 1990, or 1.8% of all deaths in Holland. There were 400 cases of assisted suicide, or 0.3%. An additional 1,000 or 0.8% of the cases were identified as involving nonvoluntary euthanasia of persons who had not given informed consent. Thus, one-third of those who received euthanasia did not meet the first two conditions of the Dutch guidelines. Cases in which physicians administered opioids in large doses to patients with the intent of ending their lives were not included in the number of cases reported under the category of euthanasia. These amounted to between 7,560 and 8,716 cases, or two to three times the number of cases of euthanasia reported. [See Paul J. Van der Maas, Johannes J.M. van Delden, Loes Pijenborg, Caspar W.N. Looman, "Euthanasia and Other Medical Decisions Concerning the End of Life," *Lancet* 338 (1991): 669-74; Johannes J.M. van Delden, Loes Pijenborg, Paul J. van der Maas, "The Remmelink Study: Two Years Later," *Hastings Center Report* 23(6) (1993): 24-27.]

A more recent report published in 1996 indicates that the incidence of doctor-assisted deaths in the Netherlands is rising. In 1995 the rate increased to 2.3-2.4% of all deaths in Holland from 1.8% in 1991. The rate of physician-assisted suicide remained steady. The rate of involuntary euthanasia decreased slightly to 0.7%, but remains significant. [See Paul J. van der Maas, Gerrit van der Wal, Ilinka Haverkate, Carmen L.M. de Graaff, John G.C. Kester, Bregje D. Onwuteaka-Philipsen, Agnes van der

Heide, Jacqueline M. Bosma, Dick L. Willems, "Euthanasia, Physician-Assisted Suicide, and other Medical Practices Involving the End of Life in the Netherlands, 1990-1995," *New England Journal of Medicine* 335(22) (1996): 1699-1705.]

About 18% of cases of assisted death were reported to the coroner in the 1990 study. The study published in 1996 indicates that more cases of physician-assisted death are reported, amounting to 41%, but most still are not. Cases in which physicians actively brought about death without the patients's consent were rarely reported. Two such cases were reported in 1990 and three in 1995. [See Gerrit van der Wal, Paul J. van der Maas, Jacqueline M. Bosma, Bregje D. Onwuteaka-Philipsen, Dick L. Willems, Ilinka Haverkate, Piet J. Kostense, "Evaluation of the Notification Procedure for Physician-Assisted Death in the Netherlands," *New England Journal of Medicine* 335(22) (1996): 1706-1711.]

The Remmelink report indicated that in 1990, some 9,000 patients asked for euthanasia, and fewer than one-third of these were acted upon by physicians. Physicians, it can therefore be surmised, play a major role in deciding which patient requests will be honored. The main reasons that patients ask for euthanasia, according to the Report, are general weakness or tiredness, dependence or being in need of help, loss of dignity, and pain (including discomforting symptoms such as chronic nausea and incontinence). Cancer was the diagnosis in 70% of those making a request for euthanasia, neurological disorder in 10%, and chronic obstructive lung disease in most of the remainder. The 1996 study indicates that there were 9,700 requests for euthanasia or assisted suicide at a particular time in 1995, a nine percent increase from the 1990 number. Of these approximately 38% were granted, a slight increase. Physicians decided not to provide assisted suicide/euthanasia in approximately two-thirds of these cases.

The Dutch courts are receiving a growing number of cases in which euthanasia is administered to those unable to ask for it, such as severely impaired newborns. In such cases, the courts have tended to acknowledge that the guidelines have been violated, but have not penalized the physicians involved. [*See American Medical News*, December 4, 1995, p. 4.] ■

Committee Members Who Developed This Report

The following members of the Committee on Medical Ethics, Episcopal Diocese of Washington, wrote, researched, edited, or otherwise assisted in developing this report.

Jean Galloway Ball, J.D., is an Elder Law attorney in private practice in the Washington, D.C. area. She often counsels clients on the legal aspects of and tools for medical decision making and end of life decisions. Ms. Ball received her undergraduate degree from the University of California at Berkeley and her juris doctor degree from George Washington University National Law Center. She is a member of the National Academy of Elder Law Attorneys.

The Rev. David Bird, Co-Chair of the Committee on Medical Ethics of the Diocese of Washington, is rector of Grace Church, Georgetown and co-author of *Receiving the Vision: The Anglican-Roman Catholic Reality Today.* Previously, he served as canon theologian of the Diocese of Pittsburgh, rector of St. Andrew's Church, New Kensington, Pennsylvania, and taught theology at Duquesne University.

Priscilla Cherouny, M. Div. is the mother of four grown children and the grandmother of two little granddaughters. She is a graduate of the Virginia Theological Seminary and has served on the staff of several parishes and as a chaplain in hospitals and nursing homes in the Washington metropolitan area. She currently ministers to four area nursing homes and is the Pastoral Assistant at St. James Episcopal Church in Potomac, Maryland.

Cynthia B. Cohen, Ph.D., J.D., Chair of the Committee on Medical Ethics of the Diocese of Washington, is a Senior Research Fellow at the Kennedy Institute of Ethics at Georgetown University. She has also served as Associate for Ethical Studies at The Hastings Center, chaired a university philosophy department, taught medical ethics at two medical schools and served as associate to a hospital legal counsel. She has written and edited several books, including *Casebook on the Termination of Life-Sustaining Treatment and the Care of the Dying.*

Frank W. Cornett, M.D., J.D. is a physician and an attorney who currently practices medicine and works as a consultant in medical malpractice in Washington, D.C. He grew up in Nevada and attended college and medical school at the University of Nevada. He studied law at the University of California, Berkeley, and Harvard Law School. He first became interested in medical ethics, especially from a Christian and Anglican standpoint, while in college.

Alex Hagerty is married and has two children. He works as a manufacturer's representative. He is captain of the Arlington County Volunteer Fire Department, where he is a certified Emergency Medical Technician (EMT), firefighter, and emergency vehicle operator. He joined the Committee on Medical Ethics because of morally ambiguous situations he encountered as a volunteer fireman. Concern for what do-not-resuscitate orders mean and their effect on rescue personnel brought him to the committee.

Patricia Lusk, M.P.H., R.N.C., L.N.H., is Director of Adult and Geriatric Health, Prince George's County Health Department, Maryland. As a registered nurse and director of a nursing home licensing program, she finds it impossible not to be concerned about the galloping advance of technology and the omission of ethical considerations in the current health care system and future health planning. She is hopeful that the work of the Committee on Medical Ethics of the

Diocese of Washington will help to raise significant bioethical issues for public dialogue.

Virginia Oler, M.D., after finishing high school in Swarthmore, Pennsylvania, was graduated from the College for Women at the University of Pennsylvania in 1945. She was graduated from the School of Medicine in 1949, interned at the Hospital of the University of Pennsylvania, and served there as a Fellow in Gastroenterology. In 1952, she moved to Washington with her husband, Wesley M. Oler, M.D., an internist, and she worked for the D.C Maternal Health and Child Welfare service until she had her family. She has completed several bioethics courses at the Kennedy Institute of Ethics at Georgetown University and at Wesley Theological Seminary.

Dorothy Rainey is a layperson at St. John's Church, Lafayette Square, Washington, D.C., with a long-standing interest in bioethics issues. She has served on the vestry and many other committees of the church. World War II interrupted her college education at the University of Montana, where she was an English major. She married a career Naval officer, raised a family, and, in the course of many moves, was always active in local Episcopal churches. She worked for several years at the Kennedy Institute of Ethics at Georgetown University in Washington, D.C., first as a volunteer, then as administrative assistant. She is currently the secretary of the Committee on Medical Ethics of the Diocese of Washington, D.C.

The Rev. George Timberlake is a chaplain at the U.S. Soldiers' and Airmen's Home, Washington D.C. His primary work is in the long-term nursing facility where he serves on the Interdisciplinary Committee to plan care of residents. He has also been active in the Alcohol and Drug Abuse Program. He has served on the Bioethics Committee of the Home since its inception in 1987 and for the past two years has chaired that committee. Mr. Timberlake is a graduate of Kenyon College and Bexley Hall. He was ordained into the priesthood of the Episcopal Church in 1950. He received a Master's of

Theology degree from Western Theological Seminary in 1969.

The Rev. Joseph Trigg is the Rector of Christ Church, Port Tobacco Parish, La Plata, Maryland and teaches in an adjunct capacity at the Virginia Theological Seminary. He has also taught in the Early Christian Studies Department at the Catholic University of America. He earned a doctorate in the History of Christianity at the University of Chicago Divinity School, where his principal focus was on early Christian theology and ethics. He is the author of books on Origen and early biblical interpretation, as well as translations, articles, and reviews in academic and church-related publications.

For further information, contact Dr. Cynthia B. Cohen, Episcopal Church House, Mount St. Alban, Washington, D.C. 20016-5094. Phone: (800) 642-4427 or (202) 537-6555 ■